The Resurrection and the Life

by
John MacArthur, Jr.

WORD OF GRACE COMMUNICATIONS
P.O. Box 4000
Panorama City, CA 91412

Library of Congress Cataloging-in-Publication Data

MacArthur, John F.
 The Resurrection and the life.

 (John MacArthur's Bible studies)
 1. Bible. N.T. John XI—Criticism, interpretation,
etc. I. Title. II. Series: MacArthur, John F. Bible
studies.
BS2615.2.M29 1986   226'.506   85-29863
ISBN 0-8024-5091-1 (pbk.)

     1 2 3 4 5 6 7 Printing/GB/Year 90 89 88 87 86

Printed in the United States of America

Contents

These Bible studies are taken from messages delivered by Pastor-Teacher John MacArthur, Jr., at Grace Community Church in Panorama City, California. These messages have been combined into a 4-tape album entitled *The Resurrection and the Life*. You may purchase this series either in an attractive vinyl cassette album or as individual cassettes. To purchase these tapes, request the album *The Resurrection and the Life* or ask for the tapes by their individual GC numbers. Please consult the current price list; then, send your order, making your check payable to:

WORD OF GRACE COMMUNICATIONS
P.O. Box 4000
Panorama City, CA 91412

Or, call the following toll-free number:
1-800-55-GRACE

1
Sickness for the Glory of God

Outline

Introduction
A. The Rejection of the Lord
B. The Resurrection of Lazarus
   1. Its importance
   2. Its intentions
      a) It points to the deity of Christ
      b) It confirmed the faith of the disciples
      c) It led directly to the cross

Lesson
I. The Critical Man
   A. His Illness
   B. His Identity
      1. His name
      2. His residence
      3. His sisters
II. The Concerned Sisters
   A. The Request
      1. Its cause
      2. Its character
         a) The attitude of humility
         b) The assurance of love
         c) The acknowledgement of humanity
            (1) The expression of Christ's love
            (2) The empathy of Christ's love
   B. The Reply
      1. The stated purpose
      2. The sovereign prerogative
   C. The Response
      1. The defense of Christ's love
      2. The delay for God's glory
III. The Cringing Disciples

Introduction

The first sixteen verses of John 11 set the background for the miracle of raising Lazarus from the dead. In verse 4, Christ reveals that Lazarus's sickness was "not unto death, but for the glory of God, that the Son of God might be glorified by it." God desired to receive glory through that miracle. Its purpose was not so much to restore the life of Lazarus, nor for the love of Mary and Martha, as it was for the glory of God and His Son. It was the most astounding of all the miracles Jesus had performed up to that point and the greatest manifestation of His glory yet seen. Jesus raised Lazarus from the dead so men might recognize Him as God through His display of divine power.

A. The Rejection of the Lord

It is fitting, after the intense rejection Christ has experienced in John 10, to see His glory still blazing amidst the resistance of the religious leaders. In John 11, Satan again fails to dim the light of Jesus Christ. The third chapter of John tells us that light came "into the world, and men loved darkness rather than light, because their deeds were evil" (v. 19). In the first chapter, John records the fact that even though the world rejected the light (vv. 10-11), the world could not overcome it (v. 5). Satan couldn't stop the plan of God from being carried out by Christ—and he still can't. Jesus says in Matthew 16:18, "I will build my church, and the gates of [hell] shall not prevail against it." Nothing can dim the blazing glory of Jesus Christ. Even though He met with incessant opposition and hate, His glory was still obvious. Chapter 11 gives the impression that the Father is so jealous of the Son's glory He makes this miracle happen so He can vindicate Jesus' honor and glory in view of the world's hatred. He jealously guards the honor of the Son. Anyone who refuses to honor the Son is removed from the presence of God to spend the rest of eternity in hell. That is a solemn reality. In fact, Hebrews 10:31 says, "It is a fearful thing to fall into the hands of the living God."

B. The Resurrection of Lazarus

1. Its importance

By chapter 11, we have already seen six miracles in John's gospel: Jesus turned water to wine (John 2:1-11), healed a nobleman's son (4:46-54), healed a lame man (5:1-9), multiplied loaves and fishes to feed over five thousand (6:5-13), walked on water (6:16-21), and cured a man born blind (9:1-7). The raising of Lazarus is number seven. Since seven is the perfect number in Hebrew thinking, it is no coincidence that this seventh miracle is climactic. The resurrection of Lazarus was the greatest demonstration of Christ's divine power during His ministry. Although He had raised Jairus's daughter (Mark 5:22-24, 35-43) and the son of a widow who lived in Nain (Luke 7:11-15), those resurrections occurred immediately after death. In the case of Lazarus, the miracle was even more monumental because Lazarus had been in the grave four days, and the process of decomposition had begun.

2. Its intentions

The miracle of Lazarus's resurrection revealed God's glory. That was always the primary purpose of miracles. In chapter 9, the disciples ask about what has caused a particular man to become blind: "Master, who did sin, this man, or his parents, that he was born blind? Jesus answered, Neither hath this man sinned, nor his parents, but that the works of God should be made manifest in him" (vv. 2-3). The miracle of chapter 11 gives glory to God for three reasons.

a) It points to the deity of Christ

Only God can give life. Jesus had been claiming to be God, and now He gives life. He said, "I am the bread of life" (John 6:35) after He multiplied bread and fed a multitude (John 6:5-14). Jesus said, "I am the light of the world" (John 9:5), and then He gave light to blind eyes and a darkened soul (John 9:6-7, 35-38). In John 11, Jesus says, "I am the resurrection, and the life" (v. 25), and then He gives life to Lazarus, who had died (vv. 41-44). This miracle glorifies God because it vindicates all the claims of Christ's deity. He was not just a man or merely a sub-god; He was God Himself in human flesh.

b) It confirmed the faith of the disciples

Jesus was glad Lazarus had died because Lazarus's resurrection would cause the disciples' faith to take a giant leap forward as they witnessed His power over death.

c) It led directly to the cross

You ask, "How could the cross bring glory to God?" Of all the events in the life of Christ, the cross brought the greatest glory to God. Jesus said, "The hour is come, that the Son of man should be glorified" (John 12:23). When the Jews and Romans put Him on a cross, the world thought that was the end of Him. Yet bearing the sins of the world on the cross brought Christ glory.

John 11 falls into four parts: the preparation for the miracle (vv. 1-16), the arrival of Jesus (vv. 17-37), the miracle itself (vv. 38-44), and the results (vv. 45-57). Let's begin with the preparation as we examine four sets of characters: the critical man; the concerned sisters; the cringing disciples; and the confident Christ, who remains in calm control while everyone else is in an uproar.

Lesson

I. THE CRITICAL MAN (vv. 1-2)

A. His Illness (v. 1a)

"Now a certain man was sick, named Lazarus."

The fact of this man's sickness is mentioned first because it is the necessary vehicle for bringing glory to God. This is not the story of Lazarus; it is the story of Jesus and His resurrection power. Lazarus just happened to be the person who was raised. So the emphasis in the verse is the sickness of Lazarus. The verse doesn't say, "There was a wonderful man named Lazarus who was sick." Rather, it says, in effect, "There was a man who was sick—he just happened to be Lazarus."

B. His Identity (vv. 1b-2)

"Lazarus, of Bethany, the town of Mary and her sister, Martha. (It was that Mary who anointed the Lord with ointment, and wiped his feet with her hair, whose brother Lazarus was sick.)"

1. His name

    Lazarus is a significant name for this man. It comes from the Hebrew name *Eleazer*, which means "one whom God helps." It is a fitting name for Lazarus because he got as much help as one could possibly get from God—resurrection.

    The Lazarus of John 11 is not the Lazarus of Luke 16, who was a beggar. They just happen to have had the same common name.

2. His residence

    Lazarus lived in Bethany. There were two Bethanys—one about two miles from Jerusalem and another (also called Bethabara) on the east side of the Jordan River. In fact, it's very likely that Jesus had returned to the Bethany east of the Jordan (John 10:40; cf. 1:28), and He was there when the message of Lazarus's sickness reached Him.

    Lazarus, Mary, and Martha lived in the Bethany that was less than two miles from Jerusalem. And that insignificant village was about to be the stage for a display of blazing glory. The greatest attestation to the deity of Christ that had yet been seen was going to take place in the village of Bethany.

3. His sisters

    It is unusual that Mary is mentioned before Martha, since Mary is the younger. Normally the older would be mentioned first. But in this case the younger is, since Mary was better known. Verse 2 reminds the reader of her identity: "It was that Mary who anointed the Lord with ointment, and wiped his feet with her hair, whose brother Lazarus was sick." John alludes to that humble act of love for Jesus in chapter 11, although he doesn't explain it until chapter 12. You ask, "Why would he allude to something he hadn't told them about?" John wrote his gospel several years after Matthew, Mark, and Luke had written theirs. The readers were already familiar with the story of Mary's anointing Jesus.

    Jesus spent many hours in the home of Mary, Martha, and Lazarus. Their house served as a haven from the hatred of the Jewish leaders in Jerusalem. It was probably the closest thing to a home that Jesus had in Judea. He loved Lazarus and his two sisters, and they loved Him.

Lazarus was critically ill. But he was also "critical" in another sense: He was going to be instrumental in manifesting the glory of God and strengthening the testimony of doubting disciples. He would be the object of the miracle that led to the cross (John 11:53).

II. THE CONCERNED SISTERS (vv. 3-6)

A. The Request (v. 3)

"Therefore, his sisters sent unto [Jesus], saying, Lord, behold, he whom thou lovest is sick."

1. Its cause

   Lazarus was dying. The Greek word for "sick" implies that his sickness was very serious. Death threatened, so the sisters immediately thought of Jesus, who had healed many strangers and certainly would come to the aid of one He loved. The wicked plotting of the Jewish leaders had caused Jesus to escape for His life to the east side of the Jordan. Realizing He could heal Lazarus, the two sisters sent a message to Him. Their faith in His healing power is evident from John 11:21, where Martha says, "Lord, if thou hadst been here, my brother [would not have] died." In verse 32, Mary says the same thing. Both of them wanted Him there because they knew what He could do.

2. Its character

   a) The attitude of humility

      The message Mary and Martha sent to Jesus is beautiful. Their statement about their sick brother, who was loved by the Lord, had a tender, humble simplicity. There was no mention of symptoms. They didn't even ask Him to do anything—they didn't say, "Here's the problem, Lord. Please do something about it." Rather, they merely informed Jesus that the one He loved was sick. They didn't tell Him what to do. They exemplified an attitude of love and faith that presented only the need. What humility!

      How do you talk to God? Do you say, "God, I have a need. Now let me tell You how to work it out: If You'll do so-and-so, things will turn out all right"?

You don't need to do that. Just tell Him your need. That's all it takes. Like Mary and Martha, surrender your needs to Christ's love, saying, "Here's my need, Lord. I'm going to leave it with You."

b) The assurance of love

Mary and Martha didn't say, "Lord, You know our brother—the one who really loves You? He's sick." They didn't try to put Him on the spot. Rather, they said, "Lord, the one You love is sick." The latter statement carries much more weight. If your love for Jesus activated His blessing on your behalf, you would be blessed on an irregular basis. If Christ operated in my life on the basis of my love for Him, I would be in sad shape because my love is inconsistent and at times self-centered.

Jesus is not motivated to come to your aid because you love Him; He helps you because He loves you. That's good to know. No matter what our problems might be, He always operates in our lives on the basis of His unconditional love. (However, that's no excuse for exploiting His love by intentionally sinning.) It's a comfort to know that God does not bless us in proportion to our love for Him. Rather, everything we have is ours because He loves us, even though we don't deserve it. What a thrilling thought! In fact, even when our love wanes and we sin, He continues to love us by chastening us. He loves us so much He blesses us even when we don't deserve His blessing. If He acted on the basis of our love, we would be powerless and without resource or blessing. Fortunately, He doesn't.

c) The acknowledgement of humanity

(1) The expression of Christ's love

There are several words for *love* in ancient Greek: *erōs*, which means "sexual love"; *agapē*, which means "divine, supernatural love"; and *philia*, which means "human affection" or "brotherly love." Verse 3 uses the verb form of *philia*, which implies that not only was Jesus God, but He was also a man. He affectionately loved Lazarus, and the sisters knew that.

There are probably many people you love as friends. Jesus also needed to express and receive that kind of love, because He was a man. It's obvious that Jesus expressed a divine love as the Savior of the world. But from a human standpoint, there were certain ones He had a special affection for. As a man, Jesus loved the companionship of Lazarus. John 11:35-36 records an expression of that love: "Jesus wept. Then said the Jews, Behold how he loved him!"

(2) The empathy of Christ's love

You say, "What's the significance of knowing Christ can love on a human level?" Jesus needed the fulfillment of human love. As a man, He needed to love and be loved. Consequently, He understands our need for love. When you're lonely and you feel there's no one you can love or anyone who loves you, know that you can say, "Lord, You know how I need love." He'll understand, because Lazarus filled His need for love. Whatever you are facing, realize that He experienced the same kinds of things (Heb. 4:15-16). Trust in Him. Somewhere there's a Mary, a Martha, or a Lazarus for you to love and be loved by. Jesus knows you need that. You say, "How do you know He'll do that for me?" Because He holds back no good thing from His children (Ps. 84:11). He became a man so He might feel what we feel. Hebrews tells us that we have a sympathetic High Priest in the person of Christ (Heb. 4:15).

Verse 3 also reveals that Mary and Martha went right to the source for help. They knew where to go. If you have a problem, go straight to the Lord. "God is our refuge and strength, a very present help in trouble" (Ps. 46:1). When the Israelites murmured in the wilderness, Moses prayed to the Lord (Num. 11:11). When John the Baptist was beheaded, John's disciples went to Jesus and told Him what had happened. They knew where to go — to Jesus, the source of all our help.

Those are good examples for us to follow because "we have not an high priest who cannot be touched with the feeling of our infirmities, but was in all points tempted like as we are, yet without sin" (Heb. 4:15). When it comes to understanding human life, wherever you are, He's been there. Peter says you should be "casting all your care upon Him; for he careth for you" (1 Pet. 5:7).

Trusting Without Tension

The sisters of Lazarus, well aware of their brother's critical condition, appealed to Jesus and left the problem in His hands. Their response reminds me of Psalm 37:5: "Commit thy way unto the Lord; trust also in him." You say, "Why does it say trusting in the Lord involves committing our way to Him?" Because most people don't. They say, "Lord, here's my problem," and then they get an ulcer. They commit their way unto the Lord, but they don't trust Him. We get on our knees saying, "O God, I have a need; here's my problem," and then we worry about how we're going to solve it. That's why these two things have to go together. Commit your way to the Lord, and then trust Him.

B. The Reply (v. 4)

"When Jesus heard that, he said, This sickness is not unto death, but for the glory of God, that the Son of God might be glorified by it."

1. The stated purpose

   Jesus, in essence, said, "The whole point of Lazarus's sickness is not death, but the glory of God." Notice that it was for the glory of God and the Son of God. You do not glorify the Father unless you glorify the Son, and you do not glorify the Son unless you glorify the Father (John 5:23). The idea of believing in God apart from Christ is not scriptural. God does not receive glory from one who is not also giving glory to the Son. They both deserve glory because both are God.

2. The sovereign prerogative

   Sometimes sickness is designed for the glory of God. Many people who are in the faith-healing movement feel that sickness is always a result of sin. That isn't always true. In John 9 and 11, sickness has nothing to do with sin. It is for the glory of God. Faith healers may reply, "But the glory of God is always greatest when there's a

9

healing." That's not always true either. Although God can receive glory from a healing, there are other times when someone gets sick but is not healed. God still can receive glory in such a case, because suffering often produces a stronger servant. Consider the apostle Paul. God never healed him. Although his infirmity in the flesh was never cured, he was a better man for it, a stronger apostle in God's service. God received more glory by Paul's illness than by his health (2 Cor. 12:7-10). So being sick can bring as much glory to God as being healed.

C. The Response (vv. 5-6)

1. The defense of Christ's love (v. 5)

"Now Jesus loved Martha, and her sister, and Lazarus."

That interjection by John in the flow of the story is important because of what comes in the next verse. It was necessary that Jesus' love for them be established before His recorded response in verse 6. Incidentally, the nature of His love for them here is revealed as divine love (*agapē*) rather than an affectionate love (*philia*).

2. The delay for God's glory (v. 6)

"When he had heard, therefore, that he was sick, he abode two days still in the same place where he was."

If verse 5 had been left out, you might have wondered if Jesus loved them because of His apparent lack of concern. But verse 5 affirms that Jesus loved Martha, Mary, and Lazarus. That helps to reassure us of Jesus' love in spite of the two-day delay. You say, "It's a strange kind of love that waits for two days before going to heal a friend who's dying." But His delay did not mean He didn't love them. Can you imagine love on the basis of time? You wouldn't say, "God, You have twenty minutes to fulfill this need and if You don't, it's clear You don't love me." That would be ridiculous. You don't measure love on the basis of time. Verse 5 tells us that the delay of verse 6 wasn't a delay of love; it was only a delay of time.

Human love would have manifested itself by hurrying to Bethany with heart pounding, but divine love wasn't in any hurry at all. What does the omnipotent Christ have to worry about? Jesus knew the delay would make His love all the more real and would bring more glory to God and more joy and faith to Mary, Martha, and the disciples. He knew a resurrection would be a better testimony to the

people than a healing. The delay—based on His love—
was important to His purposes. He wanted to wait until
Lazarus was dead so that His power might have an even
greater impact. The disciples didn't understand the delay, but Jesus did. He was setting up the great miracle He
was going to perform.

Don't worry about the wait

It's interesting to see how God makes us wait. When you
worry because God doesn't immediately come to the rescue,
realize that He often makes us wait before His love becomes
visible. Although He won't stop loving us, the fact that His
love may not be visible indicates that we may have to wait.
But remember: if you're waiting for God, that's a gilt-edge
guarantee that blessing is on the way—although it might
come in a package you're not expecting. When you pray
expecting an immediate answer but nothing happens, you
can be sure that God is preparing a blessing you might not
initially recognize. Just hang on! Isaiah 30:18 says, "And
therefore will the Lord wait, that he may be gracious unto
you, and therefore will he be exalted." You say, "Now wait a
minute; if He really wanted to be gracious to me, He wouldn't
wait so long." Not always. Sometimes God takes awhile to
wrap up all the packages the way He wants them delivered.
Don't rush Him. He loves you so much, He may make you
wait for something better than you ever dreamed you were
going to get in the beginning. Don't settle for the second
best—wait. The Lord knows what's best, and He knows the
right time; so don't ever interpret His love by time. A poet
said, "His purposes will ripen fast, unfolding every hour; the
bud may have a bitter taste, but sweet will be the flower"
(cited in William Hendriksen's *The Gospel of John* [Grand
Rapids: Baker, 1981], 2:141). The last phrase of Isaiah 30:18
says, "Blessed are all they that wait for him."

III. THE CRINGING DISCIPLES (vv. 7-10)

A. The Fear That Was Fostered (vv. 7-8)

"Then, after that, saith he to his disciples, Let us go into
Judea again. His disciples say unto him, Master, the Jews of
late sought to stone thee; and goest thou there again?"

The disciples were confused about Jesus' intentions. They
didn't understand why He wanted to return to the very place
He had just escaped from with His life. In addition, John
10:42 records that "many believed" in the area beyond the

Jordan where He and His disciples had retreated. It made more sense to them to build up their new area of ministry rather than go back to the Jerusalem area and be stoned. Furthermore, they may have thought that when Jesus said the sickness was "not unto death" (v. 4), it meant Lazarus wasn't going to die physically. If Lazarus wasn't sick enough to die, they probably wondered what was the point of going back to Jerusalem in light of the opposition there.

B. The Reassurance That Was Required (vv. 9-10)

"Jesus answered, Are there not twelve hours in the day? If any man walk in the day, he stumbleth not, because he seeth the light of this world. But if a man walk in the night, he stumbleth, because there is no light in him."

Jesus replied with a fantastic illustration. As a Christian, you don't need to fear death if you realize that God is in control of the time you will die. To the Hebrews, every day was arranged around a period of daylight and a period of night. Jesus was in effect telling His disciples, "Don't you realize that a day can't finish until it's over with? God has prescribed the bounds of My life. By all your concern for My safety, you can't lengthen it for the same reason the rejection of the Jewish leaders can't shorten it. What have we got to fear? God has fixed the calendar. Let us live out the day to the fullest because night is coming, during which no man can work (John 9:4). Jesus often said, "Mine hour is not yet come" (e.g., John 2:4), referring to the climax of the crucifixion. He knew His time wasn't up yet; He was on a divine time schedule.

Do you fear death?

Jesus' reply has great application for us. God has set the boundary on our lifetime; we'll not live a minute after or die a minute sooner. If a man is serving God, he must utilize the prescribed bounds that God has allotted for him. He need not fear any opposition if he is operating according to God's will. As a Christian, you don't need to fear death because you're not going to die before God says your ministry is through. That's a fantastic assurance. You can walk into the face of opposition with confidence.

However, there's also a serious application to an unbeliever. If you don't know Jesus Christ as your Lord and Savior, you need to realize that time is extended for no man. God set boundaries on your life too. There's just enough time to receive Christ but no time to spare.

In the legend of Dr. Faustus, which was made into a drama by sixteenth-century English dramatist Christopher Marlowe, Faustus struck a bargain with the devil. If the devil would serve him for twenty-four years, he would give his soul to the devil forever. At the end of those years, Faustus knew he had made a bad bargain. He regretfully addressed himself, saying, "Oh Faustus, now hast thou but one bare hour to live, and then thou must be damned perpetually. . . . The stars move still, time runs, the clock will strike, the devil will come, and Faustus must be damn'd" (V.ii.127). Time had run out for Faustus—and it can run out for you too.

IV. THE CONFIDENT CHRIST (vv. 11–16)

A. The Comment About Death (v. 11)

"These things said he; and after that he saith unto them, Our friend Lazarus sleepeth; but I go, that I may awake him out of sleep."

Confident of His power, Jesus spoke metaphorically of Lazarus's death as only sleep from which His friend would be awakened. Jesus knew Lazarus was dead, but He was confident He could raise him up.

B. The Confusion of the Disciples (v. 12)

"Then said his disciples, Lord, if he sleep, he shall do well."

The disciples didn't get the message. They thought Jesus meant that Lazarus was resting so he could get better.

C. The Clarification by Christ (vv. 13-15)

"However, Jesus spoke of his death; but they thought that he had spoken of taking of rest in sleep. Then said Jesus unto them plainly, Lazarus is dead. And I am glad for your sakes that I was not there, to the intent ye may believe; nevertheless, let us go unto him."

Jesus clarified that Lazarus was actually dead. He stated He was glad He was not present while Lazarus was sick. His absence allowed Lazarus to die so He could perform the miracle of resurrection and increase the faith of His disciples. They needed to have faith in Jesus' ability to give life because they would soon see their beloved Savior hanging on a cross. At that point, they would need to reach back into their reservoir of faith to believe He had power over death. They needed to learn that Christ's omniscience and omnipotence freed them from worry. Resurrection from the dead posed no problem for Jesus.

That Jesus intended the miracle to cause His disciples to "believe" (John 11:15) doesn't mean they had no faith. It means He wanted their faith to increase. An interesting thing about faith is that as you move one step up, the step you just left seems like unbelief. The disciples had some faith, but they needed more, and this miracle was going to be part of that process.

D. The Commitment of Thomas (v. 16)

"Then said Thomas, who is called Didymus, unto his fellow-disciples, Let us also go, that we may die with him."

1. Analyzed

Realizing that Jesus was determined to go back to Jerusalem, Thomas was ready to return with Him. I admire his love, but I can't say much for his faith. His love was so strong he was willing to die for Jesus, but his faith was so weak, he was sure he would. Thomas had great devotion but little faith. Before you knock his faith, however, see if you can match his love.

When Jesus was crucified, Thomas didn't die with Him. He fled like the rest of the disciples, although at that point he had good intentions. Later on, however, he did die for Christ as a martyr. He was willing to go back into the face of hostility.

2. Applied

Are we as willing to die for Christ as Thomas was? The sad fact is that most of us haven't even been willing to live for Him. Most of us live for ourselves—for pleasure, possessions, or physical cravings. Such misdirected effort is as remote as it can possibly be from dying for Jesus. Thomas said, "Let's go die with Him." We say, "Let's live for ourselves." We claim to be Christians but knock Thomas's faith when our love can't even match his.

If you want to match Thomas's love, you need to be willing to die to self; then you'll move a little closer to being willing to die for Jesus. The measure of Thomas's life was his selfless sacrifice. That's the measure of your life too. Don't tell God you love Him and then live for yourself. That kind of love is a lie. Live for Jesus Christ and be willing to die for Him. Your love won't even need to speak because it will be obvious. The measure of your love is your selflessness. We should be able to say, "Whatever the cost, my love is so strong, I'll die to self and live for Christ."

Focusing on the Facts

1. What was the resurrection of Lazarus designed to help men recognize about Christ (see p. 2)?

2. How was the resurrection of Lazarus different from the other resurrections Jesus had performed (see p. 3)?

3. What was the miracle of Lazarus intended to reveal? In what three ways does it do that (see pp. 3-4)?

4. Where did Lazarus live? Where was that town located in relation to Jerusalem (see p. 5)?

5. Who were the sisters of Lazarus? What was the youngest known for having done (see p. 5)?

6. Why had Jesus retreated to the east side of the Jordan River (see p. 6)?

7. How did the sisters express an attitude of humility regarding Lazarus's illness (see p. 6)?

8. What motivates Jesus to come to a Christian's aid (see p. 7)?

9. What is the significance of knowing that Christ can love on a human level (see p. 8)?

10. Mary and Martha recognized Jesus as a source of what? Why can we be quick to confide in Him in times of trouble, according to Hebrews 4:15 (see pp. 8-9)?

11. What was to be the point of Lazarus's sickness? Explain (see p. 9).

12. Can the Father be glorified apart from the Son? Explain (see p. 9).

13. Is sickness always the result of sin? Support your answer with Scripture (see pp. 9-10).

14. How did God receive glory from the apostle Paul's infirmity (see p. 10)?

15. Why was it necessary for John to assure his readers of Jesus' love for Martha, Mary, and Lazarus (v. 5; see p. 10)?

16. Explain how the two-day delay was important to Jesus' purposes (see p. 11).

17. Why were the disciples confused about Jesus' intention to go back to the area where He had been persecuted (see pp. 11-12)?

18. Why do Christians not have to fear death (see p. 12)?

19. Why was Jesus glad that He was not present while Lazarus was sick (John 11:15; see p. 13)?

20. Although Thomas is often criticized for his lack of faith, what did he not lack (John 11:16; see p. 14)?

Pondering the Principles

1. Jesus responded to the urgent request of Mary and Martha because of His love for them—rather than their love for Him. If Jesus were to respond to your requests based on your love for Him, would many of them get answered? Why? Read Romans 8:35-39 and praise God that you cannot be separated from His love in Christ.

2. When you are faced with a problem, do you tell the Lord but worry about the outcome? Psalm 37:5 says, "Commit thy way unto the Lord; trust also in him." When you pray about something, believe that God will answer. However, give Him time to respond according to His plan. Do you remember ever getting impatient while waiting for an answer to your prayer? Have you ever discovered it was actually a blessing that your prayer wasn't answered when and how you had expected? As you wait for an answer, trust that God will work for your good and His glory. Meditate on 1 John 5:14-15.

3. When was the last time you sacrificed time or money for the sake of Christ? How does your love for the Lord compare with that of Thomas, who was willing to die with Him? Meditate on Romans 12:1-2. Although it is difficult to hypothetically determine whether you would die for Christ in a given situation, at least consider how you are living for Him in the present. Are you willing to live for the One who made the ultimate sacrifice for you?

2
The Resurrection and the Life

Outline

Introduction
A. The Pretense About Death
B. The Promise of Life
C. The Plan of Christ
    1. Turning from those who rejected
    2. Teaching those who responded
Lesson
  I. Humiliation
    A. The Analysis of the Scene
        1. The coming to Bethany
        2. The customs of burial
    B. The Application to Salvation
  II. Revelation
    A. The Analysis of the Scene
        1. The personality of Martha
        2. The perspective of Martha
            a) The compromise of faith
            b) The confidence of faith
                (1) In the relationship of Christ to the Father
                (2) In the resurrection from the dead in the future
                    (*a*) Psalm 16:9-11
                    (*b*) Job 19:25-27
        3. The proclamation of Jesus
    B. The Application to Salvation
III. Faith
    A. Its Content
    B. Its Confession
IV. Love
    A. The Setting of the Scene
        1. Martha's confidence
        2. Jesus' calling
        3. Mary's crying

B The Sensitivity of the Savior
1. His care
2. His crying
   a) Its character
   b) Its cause

Introduction

A. The Pretense About Death

Men fear death. In fact, death is a taboo in our society. Sex used to be a widely observed taboo; now it's our national pastime, and death has replaced it. Death is the specter that haunts the end of every man's life. Our society likes to pretend that death isn't as bad as it appears by having flowers, songs, and fancy caskets at funerals. Someone even likened a funeral to a horizontal cocktail party! Man does everything he can to disguise the stark reality of death. His pursuit of money, success, prestige, position, education, and sexual satisfaction become pointless in the face of approaching death. The increasing anticipation of death leaves man with a sense of loneliness and despair. No matter what he has here in the way of security, friendship, and meaning, it can instantly vanish.

B. The Promise of Life

However, that's not how it has to be. Consider John 11:25-26. These verses contain the greatest news that has ever fallen on anyone's ears: "Jesus said unto [Martha], I am the resurrection, and the life; he that believeth in me, though he were dead, yet shall he live. And whosoever liveth and believeth in me shall never die. Believest thou this?" The greatest news is that death—because of Jesus Christ—need not mean inevitable hell. A man who believes in Him dies only that he might rise again and live for eternity. Death only opens up eternal life. That is the Christian hope, which is founded on truth.

C. The Plan of Christ

Jesus Christ conquers death in John 11. This marvelous chapter illustrates His resurrection power in the life of a man named Lazarus, in the most powerful manisfestation of divine energy that Jesus had given in His life to that point. It concludes His public ministry, which had begun about three years before. He had been proclaiming that the kingdom of God was coming and therefore Israel needed to repent from its sin. He had been performing miracles and making great statements about His own identity.

1. Turning from those who rejected

    However, Israel, for the most part, rejected Him. In John 10:31, the religious leaders intend to stone Him. In verse 39, they try to arrest Him, but "he escaped out of their hand." Their rejection ended the public ministry of Christ, who began a transition into a secluded ministry. No longer dealing with the populace of Israel, He concentrated His last days of ministry on those who had already declared their faith in Him. Jesus moved from the work of evangelizing the people to edifying His followers, who would be given the responsibility of reaching the world with the truth of the gospel. He needed to solidify their faith so His ministry would be maintained in His absence.

    Christ's focus on personal ministry to His disciples doesn't begin until John 13. Chapters 11 and 12 are the bridge from Christ's public ministry to His private ministry. Although He performs the transitional miracle of John 11 to increase the faith of the disciples (v. 15), he does it near Jerusalem in the presence of many Jews as a testimony to Israel. By it, Jesus was announcing to Israel, "In spite of your rejection, I am the Son of God." Jesus did this last miracle before the shame and suffering that He went through in His trial and crucifixion, as if to say, "Just watch and see Whom you've rejected."

2. Teaching those who responded

    The miracle of John 11 testifies to the disciples that Jesus is the Son of God in spite of their doubts. He raised Lazarus to convince them of His power over death. It wasn't to be many days until they saw Him hanging on a cross. They needed the hope the miracle could provide in order to prevent any doubts that He was the Messiah. In the process of increasing their faith, Jesus offered three levels of evidence for His power over death: First, He told them He would rise. In John 2:19, Jesus says to the Jewish leaders in the presence of some of His disciples, "Destroy this temple [a reference to His body], and in three days I will raise it up" (cf. Mark 10:33-34). Second, He said, "Let me show you a little of My resurrection power," and proceeded to raise Lazarus. Finally, He rose from the grave Himself. Following His resurrection, the disciples

19

were transformed into dynamic witnesses of the gospel. Most died as martyrs for proclaiming the truth. Having seen His resurrection power exhibited in Lazarus and Himself, they helped change the world. His power over death made such an impact on them that the central theme of their preaching was His resurrection.

John 11 is divided into four parts: the preparation for the miracle, the arrival of Jesus, the miracle itself, and the results. The preparation focused on Lazarus, his sisters, Christ, and His disciples before the miracle occurred. Beginning in verse 17, we see the arrival of Jesus at Bethany along with His disciples. They loved Him and were willing to follow Him to their deaths. Verses 17-36 present not only a historical record of resurrection life but also an analogy of the elements of salvation. Jesus is coming to a scene of death with resurrection life. Within the historical account, we will see how resurrection life applies to us, not because Jesus came to Bethany, but because He came into the world. His coming to Bethany with resurrection life parallels His coming into the world with salvation. The passage contains four basic aspects of salvation: humiliation (Christ humbled Himself and became a man); revelation (Christ declared His message); faith (man's response to Christ's work); and love (the divine motivation for salvation).

Lesson

I. HUMILIATION (vv. 17-19)

A. The Analysis of the Scene

1. The coming to Bethany

We see the humiliation of Christ in His coming to Bethany. He didn't have to come. The sisters of Lazarus didn't even ask Him to come; they only told Him that His friend was sick. He was busy with His plans. He was the Son of God, moving through the world with every minute of His time strategically clocked by God. It would have been easy for Him to say, "I'm sorry; I can't be bothered with Lazarus. After all, he's a believer anyway. He's going to rise at the final resurrection. He's in heaven right now, so there's no need to cry." Jesus could have been very indifferent, but He wasn't. He came because He was needed. He responded in humility by going back to the neighborhood of Jerusalem. Because His enemies were there, the possibility of death was very real (v. 16).

It took humility for Him to put Himself back into that position.

Furthermore, do you realize that the Son of God, the Savior of the world and Creator of the universe, was humble enough to respond to the need of two women? Jesus Christ made Himself available to them. He didn't go through the world saying, "Don't bother Me; I have important things to accomplish." Rather, He moved through humanity sensitively, meeting the needs of those He encountered. For example, when a woman who had a hemorrhage desperately grabbed His garment as He walked through a crowd, He turned around, pulled her out of the crowd, and healed her (Matt. 9:20-22). Jesus humbly moved through life, sensitive to the needs of people. That is why He came to Bethany.

John 11:17-19 says, "Then when Jesus came, he found that he had lain in the grave four days already. Now Bethany was near unto Jerusalem, about fifteen furlongs off. And many of the Jews came to Martha and Mary, to comfort them concerning their brother." Jesus arrived at Bethany, a village less than two miles from Jerusalem. It was crowded with mourners who were at Lazarus's funeral.

2. The customs of burial

Whenever someone prominent died in those days, the religious leadership came out. Lazarus must have been such a person because many people came to his funeral. People often stayed at a funeral for a week to comfort the family members. The burial took place immediately following the death because there was no way to effectively preserve the body in the heat of the region. The rest of the week was filled with mourning the deceased and comforting the family. Some people came as professional mourners, who would wail as an expression of grief. But many were there to legitimately comfort Mary and Martha. That beautiful custom needs to be more a part of our own ministry to each other.

It was customary to form a long procession that would march to the tomb. Women always led the procession because it was believed that a woman had brought death into the world by her sin, so it was thought appropriate for women to lead the mourners to the tomb. Once the group was there, eulogies were given. After returning from the tomb, they served a sparse meal of bread, hard-boiled eggs, and lentils—intended to make sure that the funeral stayed a funeral and didn't become a party.

B. The Application to Salvation

You say, "How is Jesus' coming to Bethany analogous to salvation?" Jesus came to Bethany prepared to deal with the problem of death, which is why He came into the world. The apostle Paul said that before salvation, man is "dead in trespasses and sins" (Eph. 2:1). In a sense, Christ came to mankind's funeral. When Jesus came to Bethany, it was a humble, voluntary act of His will. When Jesus came into the world, it was also a humble, voluntary act of His will. When Jesus came to Bethany, it was to deal with death on a physical level. When He came into the world, it was to deal with death on a spiritual level. Jesus came to a family in need; He also came to a world in need. He didn't have to bother with Lazarus, but He humbled Himself and came. Similarly, Jesus didn't have to bother with men, but He came and died so that He might give life to those who are dead. Just as His voluntary humiliation brought Him to Bethany to restore life, so did it bring Him to earth for the same reason. In John 10:10 Jesus proclaims to all who will hear Him, "I am come that they might have life."

II. REVELATION (vv. 20-25a)

Jesus not only came, but He spoke. He gave direct revelation from God. He uttered things innately known by Him—unlearned, but known because He was God. Everything He spoke was divine truth. When He got to Bethany, He revealed divine truth about Himself to Mary and Martha, as He did in a general sense to all of us when He came to earth.

A. The Analysis of the Scene

1. The personality of Martha (v. 20)

"Then Martha, as soon as she heard that Jesus was coming, went and met him; but Mary sat in the house."

That verse helps to portray Martha's personality. In Luke 10:38-42, Jesus visits the home of Martha, Mary, and Lazarus. Martha was the busy one, performing the duties of a hostess, while Mary was more of an introspective, pensive character. That is perhaps why, when Jesus' arrival was announced, Martha immediately went to meet Jesus while Mary remained in the house.

2. The perspective of Martha (vv. 21-24)

   a) The compromise of faith (v. 21)

   "Then said Martha unto Jesus, Lord, if thou hadst been here, my brother [would not have] died."

   Martha had probably been anxiously thinking over and over again, "If only He were here!" while waiting for Jesus to come. Then when Lazarus died, it changed to, "If only He had come." So when Jesus arrived, the thought spinning in her mind involuntarily pounced from her lips. It was a statement of half faith and half grief. You say, "That sounds like total faith. She believed that if Jesus had been there, no matter how sick Lazarus was, He could have raised him out of his sick bed." Martha believed Jesus had the power to raise Lazarus when he was sick, but not when he was dead. That's why her statement exhibited only half faith. She had confidence in Christ, yet she limited His power. She believed no illness could kill her brother when Jesus was there, but once her brother died, she thought even Jesus couldn't change that.

How full is your faith?

Before you scold Martha about her little faith, analyze your own. You may claim to believe the Lord, but then you may walk around as if you're not too sure. You say, "Lord, You've got my destiny in Your hands; I know all things work together for good, so I trust You," yet you doubt and are filled with anxiety. It's easy to trust God when everthing is going well. As long as your check comes on payday, it's easy to recognize how wonderfully the Lord provides. Your faith can be very practical as long as you're not in a situation that is out of your control. When you really have to trust God, you find the measurement of your faith. We're often like Martha. But fortunately she wasn't about to throw all her faith out the window, even though she had a little doubt.

   b) The confidence of faith (vv. 22-24)

   (1) In the relationship of Christ to the Father (v. 22)

   "But I know that even now, whatsoever thou wilt ask of God, God will give it to thee."

There was a ray of hope in Martha's statement. Although she had doubt, she wasn't about to let go of her faith. In fact, Martha turned out to be a pretty good theologian. She knew God would give Jesus whatever He asked because He had been saying that throughout His ministry. In John 6:38 Jesus says, "For I came down from heaven, not to do mine own will but the will of him that sent me." Martha knew who Jesus was. She understood His relationship to God because He had visited her home on several occasions. In fact, in John 11:27 she says, "I believe that thou are the Christ, the Son of God."

The Greek word for "ask" in verse 22 reveals more of that relationship. Rather than using the term *erōtaō*, which means "to ask an equal on an equal basis," the verse employs *aiteō*, which means "to ask as an inferior of one who is superior." That is not to say Jesus was inferior to God, because that would directly contradict Jesus' claims to be God. This verse is merely acknowledging the humiliation of Christ. You say, "If He was equal to God, why did He have to ask the Father for things?" When Jesus was in glory, before He came to the world, He was face-to-face with God and equal with Him (John 1:1). But when Jesus came to this earth, He limited the exercise of all His attributes to the Father's will (Phil. 2:6-7). He still had all His power, but He used it only in the framework of the predetermined plan of God. When Jesus came into the world as a man, He wasn't power-less; He restricted the use of His power as an act of humility. He submitted in obedience to the Father's will in every situation. In John 5:19 Jesus says, "The Son can do nothing of himself, but what seeth the Father do." (cf. v. 30). Further-more, verse 22 emphasizes His humanity from Martha's perspective.

(2) In the resurrection from the dead in the future (vv. 23-24)

"Jesus saith unto her, Thy brother shall rise again. Martha saith unto him, I know that he shall rise again in the resurrection at the last day."

You would think Martha would have been overjoyed at Jesus' reply. However, she still had doubts about His power and assumed He was talking about the resurrection of the just at the end of the world. Unlike many Jewish people of her day (e.g., the Sadducees; Acts 23:8), Martha apparently understood what the Old Testament taught about resurrection.

(*a*) Psalm 16:9-11—"Therefore my heart is glad, and my glory rejoiceth; my flesh also shall rest in hope. For thou wilt not leave my soul in sheol, neither wilt thou permit thine Holy One to see corruption. Thou wilt show me the path of life. In thy presence is fullness of joy; at thy right hand there are pleasures for evermore."

(*b*) Job 19:25-27—"For I know that my redeemer liveth, and that he shall stand at the latter day upon the earth; and though after my skin worms destroy this body, yet in my flesh shall I see God, whom I shall see for myself."

Postponing the Power of God

There's an interesting inconsistency in Martha's response. She felt Jesus could raise Lazarus at the last day based upon what He says in John 5:25-29, but she couldn't believe that He, as the Son of God, could raise him after he had been dead only four days. It's easy to rejoice in the power of God for the future while doubting it today. We often do that, saying something like, "Some day the world is going to go up in smoke, and Christ will come out of the sky on a white horse. Some day there will be a new heaven and a new earth." But when we run into a problem today, we have an anxiety attack because we fail to realize that God can also work in the present. Such reasoning is ridiculous. If you can trust God in the future, you can trust Him in the present. His power does not change. Therefore, since Jesus can handle the resurrection of all the dead (John 5:25-29), it was a small thing for Him to raise Lazarus, who had been dead only four days. Do you realize that God still has the wonderful task of raising the Old Testament saints who have been dead for thousands of years? Although their souls are with the Lord, He will raise their bodies at the end of the Tribulation.

3. The proclamation of Jesus (v. 25*a*)

"Jesus said unto her, I am the resurrection, and the life."

Notice the temporal significance of that verse. Jesus was saying, "It is immaterial whether you're talking about the past, present, or future. I am resurrection and life." What a tremendous statement! Martha projected God's resurrection power into the future, but Jesus said, "It's here right in front of you, Martha—it's Me! Time is not an issue. I will resurrect Lazarus whenever I design to do so." Jesus' use of "I am" (the Greek equivalent for the Hebrew name of God) reinforced His claim.

B. The Application to Salvation

That Christ is the resurrection and the life is precisely the message the world needs to hear. We need assurance that someone was victorious over death and has made a way for others to be victorious as well. Martha was thinking about an event, but Jesus directed her attention to Himself. Salvation doesn't come in a system of religion or an ethical code; it comes in a living person, Jesus Christ, who is "the resurrection and the life." You will not have victory over death by going to church, by thinking religious thoughts, or by doing good works. Resurrection and life are found in the person of Jesus Christ. He is the power of resurrection for the past, present, and future.

III. FAITH (vv. 25*b*-27)

The third element of salvation is faith, the response to the revelation of Christ.

A. Its Content (vv. 25*b*-26)

"He that believeth in me, though he were dead, yet shall he live. And whosoever liveth and believeth in me shall never die. Believest thou this?"

Whereas verse 25 is talking about physical life following death (resurrection), verse 26 refers to spiritual life (rebirth into eternal life). Physical death is nothing for the Christian to fear. It is merely the escape hatch into glory.

The human side of salvation is faith, which is the act of believing. "Believest thou this?" is a question for everyone who seeks assurance that they can come out on the other side of death into glory. That guarantee is valid only for those who believe Jesus is the Son of God and that He has the power that can raise them from the dead. Belief in His power to impart physical and spiritual life is what He asks of all men. Once you believe that, death is abolished. Then with the apostle Paul you can say, "O death, where is thy sting? O grave, where is thy victory? The sting of death is sin; and the strength of sin is the law. But thanks be to God, who giveth us the victory through our Lord Jesus Christ" (1 Cor. 15:55-57). Only a Christian can mock death like that, because for the Christian it is an entrance to glorification. Death cannot break the continuity of eternal life, which begins when you believe in Christ (John 17:3). You say, "What does it mean to believe?" Belief that results in salvation is a commitment to entrust one's whole self to God.

B. Its Confession (v. 27)

"She saith unto him, Yea, Lord; I believe that thou art the Christ, the Son of God, who should come into the world."

Martha believed that, but she still had doubts. Maybe you believe too, yet you still have doubts. That's a common problem because we must still struggle with the forces of evil and our human sinfulness. You may say, "I'd like to believe. What do I do?" You could read verse 27 as a prayer to God if it's the honest desire of your heart. That you might believe in Christ is the main reason the gospel of John was written. John 20:31 says, "But these are written, that ye might believe that Jesus is the Christ, the Son of God; and that believing ye might have life through his name."

IV. LOVE (vv. 28-36)

There can be no salvation without love. Love is the essential ingredient that prompted salvation and permeates every part of it.

A. The Setting of the Scene (vv. 28-32)

1. Martha's confidence (v. 28)

"And when she had so said, she went her way, and called Mary, her sister, secretly, saying, The Master is come, and calleth for thee."

After Martha had reconfirmed in her own mind that she already believed, she took off to inform her sister of Jesus' arrival. She is so satisfied with Jesus' statement in verses

25-26 that she doesn't even need to wait for a reply from Jesus to verify her confession. She had become confident of Jesus' identity and His ability to do what He claimed.

2. Jesus' calling (vv. 29- 31)

    "As soon as [Mary] heard that, she arose quickly, and came unto him. Now Jesus was not yet come into the town, but was in that place where Martha met him. The Jews then, who were with her in the house and comforted her, when they saw Mary, that she rose up hastily and went out, followed her, saying, She goeth unto the grave to weep there."

    Jesus summoned Mary to come to Him, knowing her mourners would follow her to the tomb. He had everything planned. He brought everyone connected with Lazarus out of the house and down to the tomb so they could all see the display of His glory.

3. Mary's crying (v. 32)

    "Then, when Mary was come where Jesus was, and saw him, she fell down at his feet, saying unto him, Lord, if thou hadst been here, my brother [would not have] died."

    Although Mary made the same initial comment that Martha had, she appears to have had less faith than her sister, who knew God would do anything Jesus asked. Mary's pessimism would have made her a terrific wife for Thomas—she sincerely loved Jesus, but she didn't have much faith.

B. The Sensitivity of the Savior (vv. 33-36)

    Jesus entered that cold scene of death and transformed it into a scene of warmth by His love.

1. His care (v. 33)

    "When Jesus, therefore, saw her weeping, and the Jews also weeping who came with her, he groaned in the spirit, and was troubled."

    The Greek verb for *weeping* is *klaiō*, which means "loud weeping or wailing." When Jesus saw the grief the others were experiencing, He groaned in His spirit, being deeply troubled. Sometimes the word means "angered." It could be that what troubled Jesus was His anger over sin. He was indignant about the death and sorrow that sin causes. However, I think the phrase refers primarily to an involuntary groan that was the expression of His saddened heart. He was emotionally gripped by the situation. He literally "troubled Himself," according to the Greek text. That shows He let Himself care. He could have said, "Hey, everyone, you don't need to cry; I'm going to raise Lazarus from the dead." But Jesus was torn by grief, knowing that the consequences of sin had caused death and brought sorrow into the lives of people He loved. He's a sympathetic Savior, the opposite of the image the Greeks had of their gods. They believed the gods were characterized by *apatheia*, a total inability to feel any emotion.

Jesus experienced the grief of the mourners—He let Himself care. You say, "Why did He bother?" Because He wanted to feel every pain you've ever felt and know the grief you've experienced when you've stood beside the grave of a loved one. He knows the sorrow and emptiness you felt when you watched a casket being lowered into the ground. He has even felt the pain of death that you haven't yet felt. Eighteenth-century Scottish poet Michael Bruce in "Christ Ascended" has said, "In every pang that rends the heart, the Man of Sorrows has a part."

2. His crying (vv. 34- 36)

   a) Its character (vv. 34-35)

   "[Jesus] said, Where have ye laid him? They said unto him, Lord, come and see. Jesus wept."

   Rather than using the Greek word for loud wailing (Gk., *klaiō*), John used a word that meant Jesus silently burst into tears (Gk., *dakruō*). It wasn't a professional cry or a sentimental cry; it was a spontaneous expression of love that couldn't be held back. He burst into silent tears. Those tears have been for all ages a testimony to the humanity of Jesus. He cried two other times: once over Jerusalem (Luke 19:41) and once in the Garden (Matt. 26:37). Those weren't sentimental tears; they silently coursed down His cheeks and dropped to a chest that was heaving with sighs of sorrow. He was caught in human suffering. Isaiah tells us that the suffering Messiah would be "a man of sorrows, and acquainted with grief" (Isa. 53:3). Because Jesus was so human, He

29

was trapped in the sorrow of the moment. That thrills my heart, because I know He understands grief.

b) Its cause (v. 36)

"Then said the Jews, Behold how he loved him!"

The Jewish mourners knew why Jesus was crying. They knew He loved (Gk., *phileō*) Lazarus as a friend. In another sense, that's why Jesus came into the world to bring you resurrection life—Jesus loves you. That's why He sat over Jerusalem and said, "O Jerusalem, Jerusalem . . . how often would I have gathered thy children together, even as a hen gathereth her chickens under her wings, and ye would not!" (Matt. 23:37).

This passage should help clarify that salvation begins with the humiliation, revelation, and love of Christ and that it is fulfilled in our lives as we respond in faith.

Focusing on the Facts

1. What may presently be the main taboo of our society? What taboo did it replace (see p. 18)?

2. Why does man's anticipation of death leave him with a sense of despair concerning his security, friendships, and purpose for living (see p. 18)?

3. What change in ministry did Jesus begin to make in John 11? Why (see pp. 19)?

4. What later became the central theme of New Testament preaching (see pp. 19-20)?

5. How was Jesus' humility demonstrated in His return to Bethany (see p. 20)?

6. Why did people often stay with the family of the deceased for a week after a funeral (see p. 21)?

7. How was Jesus' coming to Bethany analogous to salvation (see p. 22)?

8. How did Martha's statement in John 11:21 reveal that she lacked total faith in Jesus' power (see p. 23)?

9. What did Martha know about Christ's relationship to the Father (John 11:22; see p. 24)?

10. Before Jesus came into the world, what relationship did He have with the Father, according to John 1:1? What did He give up when He came to earth (see p. 24)?

11. Why wasn't Martha overjoyed about Jesus' promise that her brother would rise again (see p. 25)?

12. Where can true joy and pleasure be found, according to Psalm 16:11 (see p. 25)?

13. What assurance is reflected in Job 19:25-27 (see p. 25)?

14. Explain the inconsistency in Martha's response in verse 24 (see p. 25).

15. What is the message the world wants to hear about death? How does that victory come (see p. 26)?

16. What two kinds of life did Jesus talk about in John 11:25-26 (see p. 26)?

17. Why shouldn't physical death be anything for the Christian to fear (see p. 26)?

18. How is it possible to believe in Christ and still have doubts (see p. 27)?

19. What is the main reason the gospel of John was written? Cite a support for your answer (see p. 27).

20. What can we learn from the fact that Jesus "groaned in the spirit, and was troubled" (v. 33; see pp. 28-29)?

21. What is one explanation of why Jesus wept? How does that make Him different from the Greeks' characterization of their gods (see p. 29)?

Pondering the Principles

1. How fully do you believe that your destiny is in God's hands? Do you still find yourself worrying about the details of life? Do you find it easy to trust God when everything is going well but more difficult in the midst of a crisis? If so, make sure you immediately turn to the Lord for guidance and strength as you face a trial. If you are already communing with the Lord on a regular basis, that will not be difficult. If you are not praying regularly, your first reaction in a crisis will be to resolve it on your own. You need to be convinced that God cares for you and is able to bring you through any trial you may face. Meditate on Matthew 6:25-33, 1 Corinthians 10:13, 2 Corinthians 1:3-11, and 1 Peter 5:6-7.

2. Our Savior became a man and understands the sorrows and fears that we face. Therefore, we can relate to Him personally. Read Isaiah 53:4-5 and Hebrews 4:15-16. Praise God that He can identify with us through His Son and that "we may receive mercy and find grace to help us in our time of need" (Heb. 4:16;

NIV*). As a Christian, you can reflect the merciful and compassionate nature of Christ to others. Is there a neighbor, friend, or relative who could benefit from the loving concern you could offer them? Decide how you might comfort them in a practical way.

---

*New International Version.

3
Lazarus, Come Forth!

Outline

Introduction

Lesson
 I. The Perplexity
    A. Its Cause
    B. Its Character
 II. The Problem
    A. The Consequence
    B. The Cave
    C. The Command
    D. The Caution
 III. The Promise
    A. Analyzed
    B. Applied
 IV. The Prayer
 V. The Power
    A. The Command of the Lord
    B. The Coming Forth of Lazarus
       1. The proof of power
       2. The request for release

Conclusion

Introduction
God alone gives life. When Christ gave life to Lazarus, He proved beyond a doubt that He was God. That's the main point of John 11. This chapter verifies Christ's claim to be God to two groups who were present at the funeral of Lazarus. First, Jesus wanted His disciples to witness His power so their faith would be strengthened. Second, He wanted the other Jewish people who were there to witness His power

so they might believe He was their Messiah. He was performing a miracle of unbelievable power in calling the dead to life.

Jesus' claim to be the resurrection and the life is the key to John 11. He verified that claim by raising Lazarus from the dead and bringing spiritual life to some of the Jews who were watching. Many, as a result of the miracle "believed on him" (v. 45).

The Indirect Indication of Inspiration

It is significant that in a book designed to present Christ's deity, there were no qualms in the mind of the writer about presenting His total humanity. If the Bible were not true and John were trying to falsely claim that Christ was God though He really wasn't, then John certainly wouldn't have presented Jesus in the depth of His humanity. We would expect him to bypass a portrayal of Jesus that would have hindered his objective. But John does not hesitate to give a complete description of Christ's humanity in a book where he is endeavoring to present the divine nature of Christ as God in human flesh. This fact helps to verify that the gospel of John is inspired by the Holy Spirit and is therefore accurately recorded.

Lesson

I. THE PERPLEXITY (v. 37)

Let's recall the scene: Jesus had arrived at Bethany where many were mourning the death of Lazarus, who had been dead four days. Martha and Mary had wondered where Jesus had been, stating that if He had come sooner, their brother would not have died. Beginning in verse 37, Jesus encounters the perplexity of the Jews who were present: "And some of [the Jews] said, Could not this man [Christ], who opened the eyes of the blind, have caused that even this man [Lazarus] should not have died?"

A. Its Cause

Although John primarily used the word *Jews* to refer to the Jewish leaders, in this case it may refer to the people who were not followers of Christ. They were confused about why Jesus—if He loved Lazarus so much—had delayed His coming until Lazarus was dead. They could not reconcile the delay of Jesus with His power and His love for Lazarus, which they had witnessed as He wept (vv. 35-36).

The mourners had already been there four days when Jesus

34

finally arrived. In their perplexity, they wondered why Jesus had been able to heal a blind beggar (John 9), but not Lazarus, whom He knew personally. Many of those present were probably familiar with that healing because it was the last major public miracle that Jesus had done near Jerusalem. When Jesus met the blind man by the Temple, "He spat on the ground, and made clay of the spittle, and anointed the eyes of the blind man with the clay, and said unto him, Go, wash in the pool of Siloam" (9:6-7). When the man had done so, he was healed, and his neighbors reported the miracle to the Pharisees. That was a notable public miracle. Those who had witnessed could easily assume that anyone who could restore sight could take care of a disease like the one Lazarus had.

B. Its Character

Some people have suggested that the character of the Jews' statement in verse 37 is sarcastic. But I don't agree. I think those Jews were honestly perplexed because they really did believe Jesus loved Lazarus—their comment in verse 36 is very objective. They couldn't reconcile Jesus' love and power with His delay. Before you chastise them, remember that we often make the same mistake. We may say, "God, why did You let such-and-such get so far? If You had only stepped in when I asked You, we wouldn't have gotten into this mess." We become impatient and say, "God, I've been praying about this thing for thirty minutes and nothing's happened. Aren't You listening? What's going on?" Those are the kind of questions Martha and Mary were asking when they said, "If thou hadst been here, my brother [would not have] died" (vv. 21, 32). We think we trust God, but we don't always like to abide by His timing.

The Trilogy of Trust

We need to trust God by accepting His purpose and His timing. We must trust in three essentials to be an effective Christian: God's will, God's power, and God's timing. God knows what He's doing, and He knows when to do it. It's easy to waver in doubt and say, "God, things have gone too far; You're not going to be able to do anything about it now." When impetuous Peter couldn't understand why the Lord stooped to wash his feet, "Jesus answered, and said unto him, What I do thou knowest not now, but thou shalt know hereafter" (John 13:7). The Lord knew what He was doing,

35

and He would explain it at the right time. We often want to run ahead of God because He doesn't seem to be working fast enough for us. We forget God is adjusting history to His purposes. He knows what He's doing. Trust His will, His power to do His will, and His timing. He will act when the time is right— and not until. Believing that is the essence of real faith. God doesn't have to give us an account of what He does. Job 33:13 says, "He giveth not account of any of his matters." God doesn't need to turn in a time card or tell us what His calendar is. God carries out His will in His perfect power and timing.

II. THE PROBLEM (vv. 38-39)

From the standpoint of human logic, the death of Lazarus seemed like an insurmountable problem. Martha, who was somewhat pessimistic about the situation, was outdone only by her sister, Mary, who was totally pessimistic. They assumed the situation was hopeless.

A. The Consequence (v. 38a)

"Jesus, therefore, again groaning in himself, cometh to the grave."

The phrase "groaning in himself" means that Jesus was deeply moved in His inner man. It is difficult to translate because it can have so many shades of meaning. But perhaps the best translation is "indignation." Jesus was in a state of holy indignation against the effects of sin and death. He looked around and saw the sorrow and the curse of sin and experienced internal anguish. Combine His indignation over sin with His love and the anticipation of His own atoning death and you'll know why He was emotionally distraught. Jesus was no stoic; He was "a man of sorrows, and acquainted with grief" (Isa. 53:3). He stood in front of the tomb facing death, the evidence of sin's curse. His spirit was grieved, so consequently He groaned in an empathetic expression of His humanity even though He was about to raise Lazarus from the dead.

B. The Cave (v. 38b)

"It was a cave, and a stone lay upon it."

The tomb of Lazarus was a very common kind of grave in Palestine. Tombs were either natural caves or caves that had been hewn out of rock. The average size of such tombs was about six feet long, nine feet wide, and ten feet high. Inside, there were usually about eight shelves carved into the rock, three on each side and two facing the entrance. As a family member died, he would be placed in the family's tomb on one of the shelves. The body was wrapped in a linen garment and aromatic spices were sprinkled in the folds. The hands and feet were bound separately; the Jews did not wrap corpses like Egyptian mummies. The head was wrapped in a towel. The tomb had no door; a cartwheel-shaped rock sat in a groove so it could be easily sealed and removed.

C. The Command (v. 39*a*)

"Jesus said, Take away the stone."

It is significant that Jesus used men to take the stone away. Jesus was not in the business of doing tricks for public appeal. If He wanted to, He could have had that stone fly up in the air and do flips. Or He could have had it do skywriting! But Jesus didn't do things like that. Only God can raise the dead, but men can move stones.

His command to remove the stone activated Martha, who was a very outspoken individual. She impulsively reacted in fear to what He asked. Her heart was already crushed with grief over Lazarus, and the command to roll the stone away shocked what was left of her reasoning power.

D. The Caution (v. 39*b*)

"Martha, the sister of him that was dead, saith unto him, Lord, by this time he stinketh; for he hath been dead four days."

Her impulsive reply reflects the universal approach to all problems: "Oh, forget it; it can't be done!" In spite of her faith, doubt triumphed. The seriousness of the problem was just too much. Her thoughts were on the corpse. She knew the process of decomposition was accompanied by an odor. She wanted to remember her brother as he was when they had laid him in the tomb. Evidently, she thought Jesus wanted a last look at her brother. She couldn't stand the exposure of his corpse. She may have thought that since Lazarus was going to be raised at the last day (vv. 23-24) it was unnecessary to open the tomb, because they would see him again on the day of resurrection.

Martha believed it was too late for Jesus to do anything. Things seemed past His control. The Jews knew that attempting to preserve the body against the power of decay was useless. The Egyptians, on the other hand, believed that preservation was necessary and had a very sophisticated method of embalming. They disemboweled the entire body and removed the brain so there would be no internal deterioration. The body was soaked in a chemical solution for seventy days and then wrapped in bandages. Their procedures constituted a lot of effort for nothing. No amount of burial preparations can alter the state of death. Martha knew that. Consequently, she thought the corpse was an insurmountable problem, even for Jesus. She may have believed the Jewish tradition that a person's spirit floated around the body of the deceased for four days, hoping to gain a reentry. On the fourth day, because the face was no longer recognizable, it was believed that the spirit would depart. To Martha, the fourth day meant that the situation was hopeless.

III. THE PROMISE (v. 40)

A. Analyzed

John 11:40 says, "Jesus saith unto her, Said I not unto thee that, if thou wouldest believe, thou shouldest see the glory of God?" Jesus may have said that to Martha earlier. If He did, it is not recorded. He may have repeated to Martha what He had told His disciples earlier (v. 4). When the message first came to Jesus about Lazarus being sick, He said, "This sickness is not unto death, but for the glory of God, that the Son of God might be glorified by it" (v. 4). In verses 25 and 26 He tells Martha to believe in Him and His power. So He has directly told her to believe in Him and has indirectly informed her that she would see the glory of God.

Notice Jesus didn't say, "If you believe, I will do the miracle." He didn't condition the miracle on her faith. Rather, He said if she believed Him, she would see the glory of God. There's a great distinction between the two. The sovereign act of Christ raising Lazarus would have happened whether Martha believed or not. But for her to see the glory of God in the miracle, she had to have faith in Christ. She had been fighting a battle of faith and doubt, focusing her thoughts on the corpse rather than on Christ. But Christ said, in effect, "In this miracle, Martha, I don't want you to just see a corpse resurrected; I want you to see the Son of God glorified. What you carry into the miracle is what you're going to get out of it."

The theme of the universe is the glory of God. God created

everything for His glory. The only things that don't give Him glory are two groups of rebels: fallen angels and fallen men. Everything else in the universe gives glory to God. That's why Jesus said, "I want you to see in this the glory of God and Myself. I'm not nearly so concerned about what you think of Lazarus as I am about what you think of Me." The miracle of chapter 11 was performed primarily for the glory of God, not to extend the life of Lazarus, who would eventually die again anyway. Therefore, for Martha to limit her perspective to the raising of Lazarus would not have been what Christ wanted.

What is the glory of God?

The glory of God is the revelation of all the attributes of His person. For example, when Moses asks to see God's glory in Exodus 33:18, God reveals His goodness, grace, mercy, patience, and truth (Ex. 34:6). His glory is the composite of His attributes. His power to give life is just one of those attributes. When Jesus came to earth, He was the glory of God embodied. Hebrews 1:3 calls Him "the express image of his person." John 1:14 says He was the manifestation of God's glory. All the attributes of Christ revealed the attributes of the Father: You can see God's glory in the mercy, grace, goodness, love, judgment, and justice that Christ demonstrated. John 11 reveals one particular manifestation of Christ's glory: His ability to give life.

Did you know that resurrection life was one of the attributes of God's glory? Romans 6:4 says, "Therefore, we are buried with him by baptism into death, that as Christ was raised up from the dead by the glory of the Father, even so we also should walk in newness of life." The glory of the Father that raised Christ from the dead was His manifestation of resurrection power. Similarly, the miracle of John 11 is the manifestation of God's glory in resurrection power. That is why Jesus didn't want Martha to be so preoccupied with Lazarus. She was to focus on Christ and His glory. More than seeing a resurrected brother, Christ wanted her to see Him glorified. The miracle was evidence of His deity and glory.

B. Applied

Some people are like Martha: they go through life and only see the problems. They get ulcers, worries, and gray hairs over various difficulties. Then, when God solves their problem, all they see is the solution until they focus on their next problem and wait for another solution. But when a Christian keeps his eyes on Jesus Christ, he sees more than the solution; he sees the glory of Christ. Every time the Lord solves a problem, a believer can praise Him for who He is and what He has done. When we look at His glory, our lives become a manifestation of that glory. Second Corinthians 3:18 says, "But we all, with unveiled face beholding as in a mirror the glory of the Lord, are changed into the same image from glory to glory, even as by the Spirit of the Lord." What are we supposed to be focusing on in our Christian lives? Our problems? No. We are to be focusing on the glory of the Lord. When we gaze into the face of Jesus Christ as revealed in the Bible, we are going to see His glory. As a result, we will be changed into His image—His glory becomes our glory as we become more Christlike and manifest His attributes.

Is a Christian supposed to keep his eyes on his problems? No. Keep your eyes on Jesus Christ. Don't worry about your problems. If you look at your problems, you'll probably be looking only for immediate solutions. However, if you look at Christ, you will see His glory. The problem with psychologically-oriented preaching is that it focuses on problems. But if you focus on Jesus Christ, whatever happens will enable you to see His glory. His glory becomes your glory as the Spirit of God transforms you into His image. That's a great promise! I'm not interested in dwelling on problems; I want to see the glorious attributes of God.

IV. THE PRAYER (vv. 41-42)

After requesting that the stone be taken away from the tomb, Jesus offered a prayer to the Father—not a petition, but a prayer of thanksgiving. Verse 41 says, "Then they took away the stone from the place where the dead was laid. And Jesus lifted up his eyes, and said, Father, I thank thee that thou hast heard me." He didn't ask the Father for anything; He simply thanked Him for having heard Him.

You may ask, "Why was Jesus praying out loud like that?" Verse 42 tells us why: "And I knew that thou hearest me always; but, because of the people who stand by I said it, that they may believe that thou has sent me." Jesus' great claim throughout His ministry was that He had been sent from God. As God in human flesh, He was publicly announcing that He and God were one. He was praying, "Father, it's wonderful to know that You and I have already agreed on this situation and that You always hear Me because I always ask according to Your will." He didn't have to ask God for the power or right to raise Lazarus; He already had both. He didn't have to ask the Father what He wanted because He too was God, although distinct from the Father. Could any man other than Christ say that to God? No. That would be the epitome of egotism because man and God don't agree on everything. If Christ was not God, such a statement would have been blasphemous. So Jesus prayed out loud because He wanted the people present to know He was intimately connected with the Father.

V. THE POWER (vv. 43-44)

A. The Command of the Lord (v. 43)

"And when he thus had spoken, he cried with a loud voice, Lazarus, come forth."

Jesus had prepared the onlookers for His display of power. Everyone was standing in anxious anticipation of the tomb's being opened. This was a critical moment, because if Lazarus didn't come out, Jesus' credibility was on the line. The people must have immediately wondered whether Jesus' command for death to give up its victim would be obeyed or not. Panic must have filled their hearts. Did he have the power to reverse death and bring Lazarus out of the tomb? Did He have the power to recreate fresh skin and organs?

Jesus "cried" (Gk., *ekraugasen*) with a loud voice. That Greek verb was used to describe the shouting of a multitude and therefore implies an extremely loud utterance. You may say, "Why did He shout so loud?" The Bible doesn't say, but there are three possible reasons. First, in keeping with the portrayal of death as a deep sleep, it may have seemed appropriate to shout to release Lazarus from it. Second, a loud shout was commensurate with the power required for a resurrection. Third, I think Jesus shouted to alert the people that what was going to happen would happen because He had commanded it. The three words "Lazarus, come forth" would associate the resurrection with His divine power. In fact, Christ had so much power, every grave on earth would have split open had He not directed His power by specifically commanding Lazarus of Bethany to rise!

Someday, if we die before we are raptured, our bodies will be resurrected as Lazarus's body was. They will come out of the grave and be united with our souls when Christ returns for the church. First Thessalonians 4:16-17 says, "For the Lord himself shall descend from heaven with a shout, with the voice of the archangel, and with the trump of God; and the dead in Christ shall rise first; then we who are alive and remain shall be caught up together with them in the clouds, to meet the Lord in the air." When Christ comes to collect the church, He will give a shout (possibly the command "Come forth"). Then the bodies of all believers—even those who have been dead for two thousand years—will come out of the grave as new resurrected bodies. What power that will take! We can't even fathom such power.

B. The Coming Forth of Lazarus (v. 44)

   1. The proof of power (v. 44*a*)

      "And he that was dead came forth."

      The people stood by, hearts pounding in anticipation. They must have been relieved as well as shocked to see Lazarus walk out of the tomb wrapped in grave clothes. At the sound of Christ's voice, death yielded up its lawful captive, and Christ stood as the conqueror of sin, Satan, and death. The book of Revelation says He has "the keys of hades and of death" (1:18), and He unlocks death for those who believe in Him. His raising of Lazarus from the dead is absolute proof that He has power over death.

   2. The request for release (v. 44*b*)

      "Bound hand and foot with graveclothes; and his face was bound about with a cloth. Jesus saith unto them, Loose him, and let him go."

      Since each leg and arm had been wrapped individually, it wouldn't have been any problem for Lazarus to get up and walk. Imagine him wrapped in bandages and his head covered with a separate cloth—what a vivid and unique picture that must have been!

      Jesus instructed the bystanders to remove the grave clothes as if to say, "Now let's not stand around and ask him how he feels or get into a theological debate. Untie him and let him go. When you get back to the house you can talk about it." Can you imagine the apprehensive anticipation of those who removed the bandages and found Lazarus completely restored? He was alive!

Conclusion

There are some important lessons in this passage. In the commands for the bystanders to roll away the stone and unwrap Lazarus we learn that although only God can raise the dead, He still uses men to do the things they are capable of doing. That's how the Lord always operates. He does what He does, but we do what we can do. There's no greater joy in the world than rolling away gravestones and taking off grave clothes for the Lord! We play a part in what He does. The ministry we do for the Lord is an honored privilege not given even to angels.

Another truth from this passage is that if Christ can raise Lazarus from the dead by saying, "Lazarus, come forth," we can be assured that when Jesus returns and says to His own, "Come forth," we will come forth to be gathered to Him forever. That's our hope. When Jesus said, "I am the resurrection, and the life" (John 11:25), He wasn't making idle conversation. He was proclaiming an eternal truth, which he verified by demonstrating His power over death in raising Lazarus. Someday He's going to verify that in our lives. According to the apostle Paul, on that day "this corruptible shall have put on incorruption, and this mortal shall have put on immortality, then shall be brought to pass the saying that is written, Death is swallowed up in victory" (1 Cor. 15:54). Believers will experience eternal resurrection life. No more will we wear the old grave clothes of sin and death; rather, we will be in clean white linen (Rev. 19:8). Someday we will walk in heaven with Christ, because He is the resurrection and the life. May our eyes be constantly fixed on Him, and may we be "changed into the same image from glory to glory, even as by the Spirit of the Lord" (2 Cor. 3:18).

Focusing on the Facts

1. What is the main point of John 11 (see p. 33)?

2. Before what two groups did Jesus want to verify His claim to be God (see pp. 33-34)?

3. What indirect evidence for divine inspiration is given in John 11 (see p. 34)?

4. Why were the Jews perplexed about Jesus? What couldn't they reconcile in their minds (see pp. 34-35)?

5. Why would many of the Jews at Lazarus's funeral have been familiar with the healing of the blind man in John 9 (see p. 35)?

6. What seemed like an insurmountable problem to Martha (see p. 37)?

7. Why was Jesus "deeply moved" (v. 38; see p. 36)?

8. What is significant about the fact that Jesus did not miraculously take the stone away (see p. 37)?

9. Why did Martha probably think it was unnecessary to open the tomb (see p. 37)?

10. Did Jesus condition Lazarus's resurrection on Martha's faith? What did Christ want her to see in the miracle (v. 4; see p. 38)?

11. Identify the theme of the universe. Explain (see p. 38).

12. What is the glory of God? What aspect of God's glory was dem onstrated in the resurrection of Lazarus (v. 5; see p. 39)?

13. How can a believer's life become a manifestation of God's glory (2 Cor. 3:18; see p. 40)?

14. What was the nature of the prayer Jesus offered to the Father in verse 41 (see p. 40)?

15. Why did Jesus pray aloud, according to verse 42 (see pp. 40-41)?

16. Why might Jesus have cried out with a loud voice in verse 43 (see p. 41)?

17. When will Christians who have died be resurrected (see p. 42)?

18. What can we learn from the fact that Jesus requested some bystanders to remove the grave clothes rather than miraculously removing them Himself (see p. 43)?

19. Because Jesus raised Lazarus, what can Christians be assured of when He returns (see p. 43)?

Pondering the Principles

1. Do you trust God's will for your life? Do you fully believe that He knows what's best for you? Do you know what His revealed will for you is? Scripture tells us that God's will is for us to be saved (2 Pet. 3:9), led by His Spirit (Eph. 5:17-18), holy (1 Thess. 4:3), submissive to authority (1 Pet. 2:13-15), and willing to suffer for living a godly life (2 Tim. 3:12; 1 Pet. 4:19). If you are fulfilling God's will in those basic areas, you can trust that anything else you do will be in accordance with His will. Psalm 37:4 says, "Delight thyself also in the Lord, and he shall give thee the desires of thine heart." If you are following the Lord's revealed will, your desires to pursue a particular career or ministry will automatically be His desires. Make sure you believe that the Lord

can bring those desires to pass and wait patiently for His perfect timing. Verses 5 and 7 of Psalm 37 say, "Commit thy way unto the Lord; trust also in him, and he shall bring it to pass. . . . Rest in the Lord, and wait patiently for him."

2. What a privilege we have as servants of the Lord. We may not be involved in a visible, dynamic ministry, but that doesn't necessarily reduce the importance of our service in the overall divine plan. God uses people who are available. At the tomb of Lazarus, Jesus enlisted some men to roll away the stone and remove the grave clothes from Lazarus. If you saw a need you could meet, and sensed the Lord's leading for you to meet it, would you be available to serve the Lord in that capacity? Or would you be so busy that it would be easy to rationalize letting someone else do it? Pray that God would open a door of ministry for you or that you would fully commit yourself to your existing ministry.

3. Meditate on 1 Thessalonians 4:13-18 by reading it a few times. Praise God for His resurrection power and the promise of eternal life. Whom can you comfort with the truths of 1 Thessalonians 4? Who needs to know about Jesus' power over death and receive the life He offers? Make plans to call, write, or visit that person this week.

4
The Plot to Kill Jesus

Outline

Introduction
A. The Rejection of Christ
B. The Review of the Context
    1. The return to Bethany
    2. The refusal to believe
    3. The requirement for belief

Lesson
I. The Many
    A. Their Comforting of Mary
    B. Their Commitment to Jesus
        1. The object of faith
        2. The question of faith
        3. The evidence of faith
            a) The context of the verse
            b) The contrast of unbelief
            c) The convincing nature of the miracle
II. The Murderers
    A. The Collaborators
    B. The Council
        1. Their identification
        2. Their inquiry
        3. Their intimidation
            a) Explained
            b) Exemplified
        4. Their intention
            a) Advanced by Caiaphas
                (1) His personality
                (2) His prophecy
                    (*a*) Expressed
                    (*b*) Explained
                        i) A substitutionary death

Introduction

A. The Rejection of Christ

John 11:45-57 contains Lazarus's response to the resurrection. In the beginning of his gospel, John said this about Jesus: "He came unto his own, and his own received him not" (1:11). The rejection of Christ by the people of Israel becomes the pattern for the rest of the book of John. After Jesus had ministered and performed miracles for about three years, faith in Him was the response of a few, and hatred and indifference was the response of the rest. Jesus Christ, the God-man, the lover of all men, the gentle Healer, the Bread of Life, the Living Water, the Resurrection and the Life, and the Good Shepherd, was finally rejected and nailed to a cross. But before universal humiliation reached its climax on the cross, God—who is always jealous for the Son's glory—designed that Christ should perform one climactic miracle in the face of all that rejection. That miracle was the resurrection of Lazarus. It was a dynamic expression of power, which reversed the death process and made a man who had been dead four days live again.

That miracle was intended to let Israel know that even if they rejected Christ, He was still who He claimed to be and able to manifest divine power. God defied Israel's unbelief by demonstrating that Jesus was God and that He had almighty power. He gave glory to Himself and His Son in this miracle of resurrection. The miracle also brought faith to the hearts of the disciples (v. 15). It revealed Jesus' identity to them and strengthened their faith, which was waning in the face of increasing rejection. The miracle had the dynamic effect of causing some unbelievers to become believers. It elicited different reactions from the people who saw or heard about it. But in fact, those first-century reactions were no different from the ways men react to Christ today.

48

B. The Review of the Context

1. The return to Bethany

Jesus returned to Bethany because he planned to raise Lazarus from the dead. It had been necessary for Him to retreat to the east side of the Jordan River because of increasing opposition in Judea. Jesus needed to protect Himself from being killed prematurely, because the time for Him to die had not yet arrived. Jesus, having received a request to come and heal Lazarus, moved toward Jerusalem to perform a miracle so public and so dynamic it couldn't be overlooked. It must have become the topic of conversation. He knew people would believe in Him because of it. But He also knew it would throw an incendiary spark on the smoldering hearts of the religious leaders who were already opposing Him.

2. The refusal to believe

It's a paradox that there is no record of anyone's denying the miracle. Evidently, not even those who opposed Christ, denied it. How could such a notable miracle have been challenged? Everyone knew Lazarus was dead, but the religious leaders had already made up their minds to reject Christ in spite of any evidence. They might as well have said, "Don't confuse us with the facts; we know He's not the Son of God. It doesn't matter if He raised the dead. That only confuses our unbelief." Rather than denying the miracle, they denied that Jesus was who He claimed to be.

3. The requirement for belief

The key to understanding the different reactions seen in John 11 is contained in verse 40: "Jesus saith unto [Martha], Said I not unto thee that, if thou wouldest believe, thou shouldest see the glory of God?" He was saying, "If you want to get the most out of this miracle and see its true value, you've got to come to it in the right frame of mind. If you come to the miracle believing it's going to manifest God's glory, then that's what you'll have the capacity to see. If you come to the miracle preoccupied with a corpse, all you're going to see is a corpse brought to life, and you won't recognize the glory of God. If you come to the miracle blinded with an unbelieving, hardened heart, you're going to walk away in confused unbelief." Whatever attitude you bring to such an event will color the decision you make about what happens. That's true of anything we experience. If you have the right attitude and an open heart, you will come to the right conclusion.

In John 7:17 Jesus says, "If any man is willing to do His will, he shall know of the teaching, whether it is of God, or whether I speak from Myself" (NASB*). God reveals truth to those who are open to it. If your mind is closed, you haven't got a chance. Both kinds of mindsets were represented at Bethany. The open hearts responded by believing and experienced love and truth. The closed minds walked away filled with hate, unable to comprehend the significance of the miracle.

The miracle had differing effects on the four groups of people that appear in John 11: Many observers believed in Jesus; the soon-to-be murderers had a new excuse to kill Him; the multitudes for the most part only watched as spectators; and Mary, Martha, and the disciples had their faith strengthened. Two of the groups were believers, and two were unbelievers. There is always division over Christ. He came saying, "I am the Son of God. I came to bring the message of salvation. I came to reveal Myself and the Father to you." If you believe in Christ, you're on the side of truth. If you don't believe in Him, you're on side of those opposing Christ. He brought a sword to divide men so that their attitude toward God might be made clear (Matt. 10:34-37). The theme of division is repeatedly mentioned in John.

Lesson

I. THE MANY (v. 45)

    A. Their Comforting of Mary (v. 45a)

        "Then many of the Jews who came to Mary."

        Lazarus and his sisters were well known. That many Jews came to mourn Lazarus's death indicates he was a prominent citizen. Although the use of the word *Jews* by the apostle John generally refers to the religious leadership of Israel, it also refers to the common people. You will notice that verse 45 indicates that they "came to Mary" but doesn't mention Martha. Evidently Mary was the most sorrowful and disconsolate of the two. Verse 31 records that the Jews comforted Mary, not Martha, who always took the role of a hostess and was preoccupied with her duties. When Jesus arrived at

*New American Standard Bible.

Bethany, Martha ran out to meet Him while the Jews were comforting Mary. In verse 33, Jesus sees Mary weeping along with the Jews who were comforting her. She appears to have needed more comfort than Martha did because of her weaker faith.

B. Their Commitment to Jesus (v. 45*b*)

"And [having] seen the things which Jesus did, believed on him."

1. The object of faith

The Jews who came to comfort Mary had witnessed an astounding miracle by Christ. As a result, "they believed on him." The key to that phrase is in the last two words, "on him." For faith to be meaningful, it must be placed in the right object. Believing in nothing in particular is not true faith. One theological perspective today emphasizes having faith in faith. An advocate of such a philosophy might say, "I believe in believing. I believe that God is in control." But faith in nothing is nothing! It doesn't mean anything to believe in believing. If you can't believe in something substantial, then your belief is ridiculous.

Faith is nothing unless it is placed in Jesus Christ. Peter said, "Neither is there salvation in any other; for there is no other name under heaven given among men, whereby we must be saved" (Acts 4:12). If a man does not put his faith in Christ, his faith is meaningless. John 1:12 says, "But as many as received him, to them gave he power to become the children of God, even to them that believe on his name." Christ is the essential object of faith for salvation. There aren't any other options. You can't believe anything you want.

It's amazing that people will affirm that God is a God of order, maintaining absolute precision in everything He does in the natural world, yet believe He is unconcerned about the moral world. The scientist in the laboratory operates on the basis that his chemical mixtures are not going to violate a known truth and blow him to bits. The astronauts who blast off into space count on the absolute immutability and accuracy of scientific laws. If God is a God of law and order in the natural realm, He's not going to say, "Oh, just do your own thing. Believe anything you want." Such inconsistency is absurd!

2. The question of faith

51

The phrase "believed on him" does not always imply genuine, saving faith. I can say, "I believe" as an expression of true faith. Someone else, however, can say the same thing and not be saved. James 2:19 says, "The demons also believe, and tremble." Although many people see Christ's miracles in John 2, Jesus does not commit Himself to them because He knows the character of their belief is not legitimate (vv. 23-25). Belief can refer to either genuine heart knowledge or mere mental assent. Christ shows the difference between the two in John 8:30-31, "As he spoke these words, many believed on him. Then said Jesus to those Jews who believed on him, If ye continue in my word, then are ye my disciples indeed." In other words, "Your initial assent to believing does not necessarily mean you've totally committed your life to Me." There are millions of people who would not deny that Jesus is the Son of God, but they don't really know Him with the kind of belief that results in salvation.

3. The evidence of faith

   a) The context of the verse

   I think the belief of the Jews in John 11:45 implies genuine salvation for several reasons. First, verse 52 states that the death of Christ, which resulted in part from the fact that He performed the miracle of John 11, would "gather together in one the children of God that were scattered abroad." Since Jesus' ministry had been primarily directed toward the nation of Israel, I believe the miracle of Lazarus's resurrection brought about salvation in the lives of some of God's chosen people.

   Second, the Jewish leaders feared that unless they got rid of Jesus, everyone would "believe on him" (v. 48). Evidently, they were convinced of the genuineness of those people's faith. Third, Jesus made the statement (v. 4) that the sickness of Lazarus was "for the glory of God that the Son of God might be glorified by it." When people believe in Him, Jesus receives the greatest glory.

   I also believe they exercised genuine faith because of

   b) The contrast of unbelief

   The reaction in the rest of chapter 11 is unbelief. Whenever Christ presented Himself, there was a

52

division of belief and unbelief. Therefore, to show that dichotomy, it is logical to assume that the beginning of the chapter deals with honest belief.

c) The convincing nature of the miracle

If a man's heart was open when such a convincing miracle happened, he most likely would have believed. May I hasten to say that the "many" refers only to those Jews who were at the funeral, not to all Israel. It was the group of Jews attending the funeral that believed in Christ.

What must you believe about Christ to be saved?

You must believe that Jesus is the Son of God and that He came into the world in human flesh to die on the cross and rise again. Now that He has ascended to the Father, He can come into your life and forgive your sins.

II. THE MURDERERS (vv. 46-54)

A. The Collaborators (v. 46)

"But some of them went their ways to the Pharisees, and told them what things Jesus had done."

This group of informers were stool pigeons for the Pharisees. They came to the miracle in unbelief and left the same way. They didn't even bother to find a plausible explanation for the miracle. They ran to inform the Pharisees of the trouble they were in.

Some commentators have assigned a pure motive to these individuals, believing they went to testify to the Pharisees. I don't think that's the case, because nothing is ever said of them after verse 46. Had they been believers, they would likely have been quizzed, like the blind beggar in John 9. Also, the fact that this section talks about the hatred of those who sought to murder Christ leads me to believe they were associated with the Pharisees. I believe they came with the sinister intention of warning the Pharisees that the crowds might follow Jesus. Perhaps they wanted to activate the leaders against Him in some way. If so, they were successful.

This is a predictable result for people who have hard hearts. You can show them the complete truth of God, but they still won't respond to it. There is no capacity in an unbelieving person to perceive the truth. As long as a person refuses to accept new information, you will be unable to communicate it to him. He can't understand because he won't understand. Someone with a predetermined unbelief doesn't even bother to rationalize, let alone investigate the evidence. The Jews who collaborated with the Pharisees didn't even worry about the miracle. Anyone who could stand by a grave, watch a man who had been dead four days walk out, and not believe is a hopeless case. That is why "no man can come to [Jesus], except the Father . . . draw him" (John 6:44). No one can come to Christ until God reaches into his heart and melts away the unbelief. Therefore, before you witness for Christ, you need to pray that God will till the soil so the Word can take root in a person's heart. Before I preach, I ask God to prepare hearts to receive truth, because a hard, unbelieving heart has no fertilized ground for faith to take root in. God has to till the soil by the Holy Spirit before a person can be prepared to receive the truth.

B. The Council (vv. 47-54)

1. Their identification (v. 47a)

"Then gathered the chief priests and the Pharisees a council."

The chief priests were ex-high priests, mostly of the politically oriented sect of the Sadducees. They were theological liberals who didn't believe in resurrection or angels. The other members of the council were the religious legalists known as the Pharisees. These two strange bedfellows got together to determine what they should do. They agreed on one thing: they wanted to get rid of Jesus.

2. Their inquiry (v. 47b)

"And said, What do we? For this man doeth many miracles."

Notice there was no denial of the miracles. You can imagine someone's saying, "Why don't we believe in Him? It seems logical to do so. We've got to admit He has done many miracles." But instead of recognizing Him, they decided to kill Him. He was a threat to the status quo.

3. Their intimidation (v. 48)

"If we let him thus alone, all men will believe on him; and the Romans shall come and take away both our place and nation."

a) Explained

The council members were concerned only about protecting their own interests. They thought that if Jesus got a big following and the people pushed Him into being a political Messiah, Rome would come down and squash the rebellion, taking away their religious and political authority.

Don't confuse me with the facts—my mind is made up!

It is interesting that the religious leaders didn't discuss Lazarus. They were unable to explain his resurrection. They were masters at ignoring miracles. Every time they tried to look into a miracle, they got baffled and humiliated. Back in chapter 9 the Pharisees ask the beggar who has been born blind how he has been enabled to see. The beggar explained that Jesus had anointed his eyes with clay and made him wash it off so he could be healed. The unbelieving Pharisees concluded He was unqualified to do anything miraculous because they didn't know where He had come from. The man who had been blind replied, "Why here is a marvelous thing, that ye know not from where he is, and yet he hath opened mine eyes" (v. 30). He couldn't believe the Pharisees didn't recognize that Jesus had been sent from God.

John 9 demonstrates the way unbelievers investigate a miracle. They start out with a presupposition and come to the same conclusion they started with by disregarding all the facts. The Pharisees ignored the fact that Lazarus had been resurrected. They were afraid they were going to lose their seats of authority and therefore refused to believe anything that might expose their darkness to the light of truth.

The Pharisees feared Rome, which was a relatively tolerant authority, because it had been known to scatter people who had been involved in insurrections. They were aware that the resurrection of Lazarus could increase public excitement over Jesus. He had been at the last two Passovers and had caused a stir. The first time He came, He cleansed the Temple. They knew such a person was a spark among the straw; they would have a political conflagration on their hands if the people idolized Jesus as they had at the second Passover (John 6:14-15). Their analysis of the situation was accurate. In John 12:13, when Jesus finally gets to Jerusalem, the crowd cries, "Hosanna! Blessed is the King of Israel" as they throw palm branches at His feet.

However, their attraction to Him was only superficial because by the end of the week they were shouting, "Crucify him!" (Mark 15:14). But in John 11, the Jewish leaders have something to fear because the people are enamored with Jesus. They decide the best thing to do is to get rid of Him.

    b) Exemplified

There is an interesting philosophy of solving problems that is popular today. Many people judge something not by whether it is right or wrong but by how it will affect them: "How will such-and-such affect my income, status, or happiness, and will it relieve the pressure I'm under?" In fact, someone told me, "You can't be a lawyer and be honest." I disagree. However, if you can't do what's right in the career you're in, then you need to get out of it. Someone might say, "I've committed many wrongs, but I haven't lost yet." The Bible says, "The Lord is not slack concerning his promise, as some men count slackness, but is longsuffering" (2 Pet. 3:9). The reason you haven't lost yet is that God is lovingly patient with you. But don't be like the people who say in the same chapter, "Where is the promise of his coming?" (v. 4). In other words, "He hasn't come yet, and He never will." Judgment may not come today, but it will come.

The Pharisees were operating on situation ethics. They wanted to preserve their own comfort. Jesus illustrates their self-serving character in the parable of Matthew 21, in which Israel is likened to a vineyard. God sent His servants, the prophets, to instruct the nation. But the religious leaders persecuted them. Finally God sent His Son, assuming those who were entrusted with the spiritual care of His nation would respect Him. But the religious leaders, according to the parable, decided to kill the Son that they might steal His inheritance. They were out for what they could get. They had no ability to discern truth.

  4. Their intention (vv. 49-54)

    a) Advanced by Caiaphas (vv. 49-52)

      (1) His personality (vv. 49)

"And one of them, named Caiaphas, being the high priest that same year, said unto them, Ye know nothing at all."

Caiaphas criticized the council for their ignorance. He was a disgusting person—an egotistical, rude opportunist. He was a godless hypocrite bent on getting what he wanted at any cost. He was the son-in-law—and puppet—of Annas, who had previously been high priest.

(2) His prophecy (vv. 50-52)

(a) Expressed (v. 50)

"Nor [do you] consider that it is expedient for us that one man should die for the people, and that the whole nation perish not."

Caiaphas didn't care about shedding innocent blood; he was the biggest hypocrite that ever was. He said, in effect, "If we don't get rid of Jesus, He will lead a rebellion. Rome will squash it, and we'll all die. So, men, either Jesus dies or the nation perishes. Don't you know that?" Caiaphas was suggesting murder under the guise of patriotism. But he was a phony. He hated Jesus, who presented a threat to his popularity, so he intended to get rid of Him. There was no threat of revolution. The Romans didn't seem too concerned when the crowds were throwing palm branches at His feet.

When Christ is brought to trial in Matthew 26:63, Caiaphas says, "Tell us whether thou be the Christ, the Son of God." Jesus answered, saying, "Thou hast said; nevertheless, I say unto you, Hereafter shall ye see the Son of man sitting on the right hand of power, and coming in the clouds of heaven" (v. 64). Caiaphas hoped Jesus would say something that would be considered blasphemous so the council could justify killing Him. Verse 65 reveals the high priest's hypocritical concern: "Then the high priest tore his clothes, saying, He hath spoken blasphemy!" In Jewish culture, people tore their clothes as a symbolic expression of sorrow or anger. As high priest, Caiaphas appeared to express indignation at the words of Jesus, but he inwardly rejoiced that he now had reason to kill Him. He feigned religious zeal and patriotism in his desire to get rid of Jesus.

Following the common strategy of presenting two extreme alternatives as if there were no other, Caiaphas pressured the council into agreeing with him. He in effect said, "Either Christ dies, or we all die." Illogical as it was to think that Rome would kill them and destroy the nation, they followed his reasoning. No one apparently raised any objections or offered other alternatives. Intimidated by his power, the council agreed to kill Jesus to save the nation, even though the nation was not in any real danger. The sad part was that killing Jesus didn't ultimately save the nation. A few decades later, Rome smashed the nation into oblivion—1,100,000 Jews were killed under Titus Vespasian. Caiaphas was wrong. Killing Jesus didn't save the nation; it destroyed it.

(b) Explained (vv. 51-52)

    i)   A substitutionary death (v. 51)

"And this spoke he not of himself; but, being high priest that year, he prophesied that Jesus should die for that nation."

The following words become a prophecy of Christ's death: "Nor consider that it is expedient for us that one man should die for the people, and that the whole nation perish not" (v. 50). That was an accurate prophecy. Christ died for the nation that its people might not perish. Out of the degenerate mouth of that high priest came the truth of God. The words he uttered in blasphemy were transformed by God into a prophecy with a deeper meaning. Caiaphas was totally unaware that He was speaking the truth of God.

I'm glad God can even take someone opposing His purposes and use him for His glory.

Psalm 76:10 says, "The wrath of man shall praise [Him]." Psalm 2:4 says, "He who sitteth in the heavens shall laugh; the Lord shall have them in derision." The council thought that by killing Jesus, they'd save the nation. Ironically, they killed Jesus and lost the nation too.

God can use anything to accomplish His purposes. He had Caiaphas unwittingly prophesy that Jesus must die. That elevated Caiaphas to the stature of Balaam's donkey. Balaam provides a good illustration of Caiaphas because he too made an unwilling prophecy (Num. 22-23). However Caiaphas made a prophecy without even knowing it. That's how God can use someone to speak His truth. Proverbs 19:21 says, "There are many devices in a man's heart; nevertheless, the counsel of the Lord, that shall stand."

Verse 51 says Caiaphas spoke "not of himself; but, being high priest that year." Historically, the high priest was God's spokesman, as Caiaphas was in this case, except he was unaware he was prophesying. The very words of evil by which Caiaphas condemned himself were the same ones the Holy Spirit used to convey the truth of God. Using the evils of Satan to His own end, God was able to use Caiaphas's own words to declare the effect of Christ's death. God uses human instrumentation—even the hatred of men. Christ's crucifixion on the cross is an enduring illustration of that. It was the worst thing men could do, yet it accomplished the greatest blessing on their behalf. Caiaphas was just a link in the divine decree. He fulfilled the counsel of God without even knowing it.

Who crucified Christ?

Who was responsible for Christ's death? Acts 4:26-28 says, "The kings of the earth stood up, and the rulers were gathered together against the Lord, and against his Christ. For of a truth against thy holy child, Jesus, whom thou hast anointed, both Herod, and Pontius Pilate, with the nations, and the people of Israel, were gathered together, to do whatever thy hand and thy counsel determined before to be done." God used the hatred of the Jews and the Gentiles to bring about salvation. The Jews and the Romans both crucified Christ. In fact, any unbelievers who ultimately reject the truth about Christ "crucify to themselves the Son of God afresh, and put him to an open shame" (Heb. 6:6). According to 1 Corinthians 11:27, a Christian can also "be guilty of the body and blood of the Lord" when he partakes of Communion unworthily. The guilt for crucifying Christ encompasses everyone. However, predetermining the outcome, God used the wrath of men to accomplish their salvation.

ii) A unifying death (v. 52)

"And not for that nation only, but that also he should gather together in one the children of God that were scattered abroad."

Jesus not only died for Israel, but for the Gentiles also—the other children of God scattered throughout the world—so He might make those groups into one. That is the great mystery of the church. Ephesians 2:14 says Christ's death "hath broken down the middle wall of partition" between Jew and Gentile. All who place their faith in Christ become one in Him: "There is neither Jew nor Greek, there is neither bond nor free, there is neither male nor female; for ye are all one in Christ Jesus" (Gal. 3:28). That describes the Christian's positional unity. Jews and Gentiles are brought together into one body, the church. Christianity is not a system of religious activities; it is actually a love relationship with Jesus Christ and other believers.

b) Accepted by the council (v. 53)

"Then from that day forth they took counsel together to put him to death."

The council concluded that the giver of life deserved death and began to plot how to do it. The people, however, weren't part of the plot until the very end, when they cried, "Crucify him!" (Mark 15:14).

c) Avoided by Christ (v. 54)

"Jesus, therefore, walked no more openly among the Jews, but went from there unto a country near to the wilderness, into a city called Ephraim, and there continued with his disciples."

The end of Jesus' public ministry was approaching. Because of increasing opposition, Jesus found it necessary to escape for His life because it was not yet His time to die (John 7:30). He was driven out of Jerusalem for the last time.

We have seen the many who believed and the plotting of the murderers. But how did the multitudes of Israel who weren't in on the plot respond to Lazarus's resurrection?

III. THE MULTITUDES (vv. 55-57)

A. The Rising Excitement (vv. 55-56)

"And the Jews' passover was near at hand; and many went out of the country up to Jerusalem before the passover, to purify themselves. Then sought they for Jesus, and spoke among themselves, as they stood in the temple, What think ye, that he will not come to the feast?"

There was an excitement brewing among the multitudes as the people began arriving in Jerusalem in preparation for Passover. Jewish law required that ceremonial cleansings be performed prior to participating in the feasts. Many wondered if Jesus would show up in Jerusalem where He would find tension in the air and be met with the boiling hatred of the Jewish leaders. He had been to the last two Passovers, and since His popularity made Him quite an attraction, the people sought Him.

Many people today have a similar attitude toward Christianity. They view it as a spectator sport—they don't participate; they just watch. Liberal churches are filled with Jesus watchers who look at Him with detached interest. They have no commitment and faith in Christ; therefore, they have no salvation and no love for others or desire to serve. They get involved in religion only superficially. Ironically, the same type of people also cried, "Crucify him!" (Mark 15:14). Jesus said, "He that is not with me is against me" (Matt. 12:30). So many people want to watch Jesus without making a commitment to Him.

B. The Requested Extradition (v. 57)

"Now both the chief priests and the Parisees had given a commandment that, if any man knew where he were, he should show it, that they might take him."

The religious leaders wanted the people to inform them of Jesus' whereabouts so they could get rid of Him. What an interesting climax to a resurrection! With a glorious display of power, Jesus restored life to Lazarus. Because Jesus was glorified through that miracle, the religious leaders felt threatened and wanted to kill Him. And that is why God had to send His Son—so that His death could overcome the depths of sin and unbelief.

Whenever Jesus displays His glory, you can expect Satan to activate his forces against Him. The pawns of the prince of darkness wanted to do away with Jesus. The people who were spectators were not much better. Once during the week they were acknowledging Him as King (Luke 19:38), and later, when instigated by the religious leaders, they were yelling, "Kill him!" (Mark 15:11-14). The fickle mob was led by the emotions of the moment. They were content just to watch Jesus, even when He was hanging on the cross.

Conclusion

There is another group present in John 11: Mary, Martha, and the disciples. Although their reactions weren't specifically recorded, I believe their faith was strengthened. On the way to Bethany to raise Lazarus, Jesus said to His disciples that the miracle was "to the intent [they] may believe" (v. 15). He desired to strengthen their faith. Furthermore, I believe the hospitality of Martha and the devotion of Mary in chapter 12:1-8 demonstrates that their faith had been strengthened.

How do you react to Christ? Do you believe in Him? Do you reject Him as that second group did? Are you one of the crowd that hangs around just to watch? Or are you a Christian who has now had your faith strengthened by seeing Christ display His power in John 11? What's your reaction to the miracle of resurrection?

Focusing on the Facts

1. Rather than denying the miracle of Lazarus's resurrection, what did the religious leaders deny (see p. 49)?

2. Explain how the attitude of a person's heart would color the conclusion he would come to about the significance of a miraculous event (see pp. 49-50).

3. To whom does God reveal truth (John 7:17; see p. 50)?

4. What is the twofold division over Christ? Why did Christ come to establish that division (see p. 50)?

5. How did the Jews who had come to comfort Mary respond to Christ (John 11:45; see p. 51)?

6. What must happen for faith to be meaningful (see p. 51)?

7. What is the proper object of faith, according to Acts 4:12 (see p. 51)?

8. Does belief in Christ always indicate saving faith? Explain (see p. 52).

9. What must a person believe about Christ to be saved (see p. 53)?

10. What is the predictable result of a hard heart? According to John 6:44, what is required before a person can come to Jesus? What should we pray for before witnessing to others about Christ (see pp. 53-54)?

11. Of whom did the council consist? What were they concerned about, according to verse 48? Why (see pp. 54-55)?

12. Why did the Pharisees conclude in John 9 that Jesus wasn't qualified to perform any miracles (John 9:29-30; see p. 55)?

13. Rather than determining if something is right or wrong, how do many people solve problems (see p. 56)?

14. Who was Caiaphas? What did he appear to be concerned about (see pp. 56-57)?

15. How did Caiaphas pressure the council into agreeing with him (see p. 58)?

16. What was the prophecy that Caiaphas gave? Explain what he meant by it as well as the deeper meaning it had (see p. 58).

17. How does the cross illustrate that God can use unwilling men to accomplish His purposes (see p. 59)?

18. Who is responsible for Christ's death (see p. 60)?

19. In what sense was Jesus' death unifying? Support your answer with Scripture (see p. 60).

20. What conclusion did the council come to after Caiaphas's prophecy? As a result, what was Jesus forced to do? Why (see p. 61)?

21. What was the reaction of the multitudes to the resurrection of Lazarus? How is that similar to what is found in many churches today (see pp. 61-62)?

22. How did Mary, Martha, and the disciples benefit from the miracle Jesus performed (see p. 62)?

Pondering the Principles

1. Saving faith is trust that has been placed in Jesus Christ. Are you trusting in His death and resurrection for the forgiveness of your sins? If you have never done so, memorize Acts 4:12 and John 1:12. Make a point of finding out what the people you converse with are counting on for salvation. Consider asking them the following question: If you died today and God asked you why He should let you into heaven, what do you think you would tell Him? On a piece of paper, list what you think would be the five most likely answers people would give. Meditate on the parable of the two builders in Matthew 7:24-27. The quality of the foundation of one's faith will determine the level of security one can experience in this life, as well as his eternal destiny. Praise God that we can know Him personally through His Son, the "living stone" (1 Pet. 2:4), who is "the same yesterday, and today, and forever" (Heb. 13:8). He is the only foundation that never changes.

2. What determines how you solve the problems you face? Is it primarily by how the situation will affect your income, status, or happiness? Or are you mainly concerned about discovering the right thing to do? The next time you are looking for a solution, immediately try to view the problem through the eyes of Christ by wondering, "What would He have done in this situation?" To do that you will need to be reading the Bible regularly and studying the life of Christ so your responses can be Christlike in character.

Scripture Index